THE
VANISHING
POWER
of
DEATH

THE
VANISHING
POWER
of
DEATH

ERWIN W. LUTZER

MOODY PUBLISHERS
CHICAGO

All Scripture quotations, unless otherwise indicated, are taken from
the *Holy Bible, New International Version*®. NIV®. Copyright © 1973,
1978, 1984 by International Bible Society. Used by permission of
Zondervan Publishing House. All rights reserved.

Scripture quotations marked NASB are taken from the *New American
Standard Bible*®, © Copyright The Lockman Foundation 1960, 1962,
1963, 1968, 1971, 1972, 1973, 1975, 1977, 1995. Used by permission.

Scripture quotations marked NKJV are taken from the *New King James
Version*. Copyright © 1979, 1980, 1982, 1992 by Thomas Nelson,
Inc. Used by permission. All rights reserved.

Cover photo: © 2003 Kevin Fleming/CORBIS

Library of Congress Cataloging-in-Publication Data

Lutzer, Erwin W.
    The vanishing power of death / Erwin W. Lutzer.
        p. cm.
    ISBN 0-8024-0944-X
    1. Death—Religious aspects—Christianity. I. Title.

BT825.L92 2004
236'.1--dc22

                                                      2003020505

                      1 3 5 7 9 10 8 6 4 2

              Printed in the United States of America

To our dear friends Scott and Janet Willis,
who eagerly await the day when
they shall be reunited with six of their children
who even now behold the face of their Father in heaven—

Ben

Joe

Sam

Hank

Elizabeth

Peter

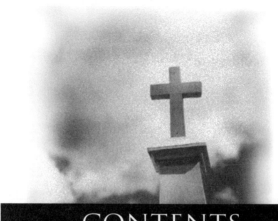

CONTENTS

THE END THAT
COMES TO US ALL

Question: How many people died in the United States the day *before* September 11, 2001?

We don't know the exact number, but we have a reasonable approximation. Every year in the United States about 3.3 million people die. Divide that by 365, and you will discover that about 6,400 people die each day from various causes: cancer, heart disease, accidents, murder, choking, drowning, and so forth.

That means, then, that twice as many people died in the United States of "natural causes" on September 10, 2001—and again on September 11 —as died in the terrorist attacks! Yes, for every person who died in the Twin Towers, that field in western Pennsylvania, or the Pentagon, two others died in our hospitals, homes, and highways.

That fact is obscured by the dramatic and heart-wrenching loss of life in lower Manhattan, western Pennsylvania, and just outside Washington, D.C. that sunny September morning. The burning Twin Towers in New York forced us to confront the reality of death on a massive scale. I was at a meeting with religious broadcasters at the Maranatha campgrounds in Michigan when the news came that a plane had hit one of the towers of the World Trade Center. About thirty of us gathered around a television set, only to see a second plane crash into the other tower. And when we watched the burning towers collapse, we knew that thousands of lives would be lost.

Death came suddenly to some, but others had their lives spared, often by a strange coincidence. There was a man, we are told, who was waiting to get into a subway car, but the doors slammed in his face. He was upset because of the delay, but because of that coincidence, he arrived at the World Trade Center just in time to see people jump from the top floors, clothes on fire.

That morning, a mother visited with her daughter, who worked at the World Trade Center. The visit delayed her daughter's intended arrival time and spared her life. Others, who diligently arrived to work on time, sealed their fate.

One man on the eighty-fourth story returned to his desk when the announcement came over the intercom that employees were to stay put. He died because he obeyed the instructions. Some of his friends ignored the command and began the long trek down the stairs. They lived to tell their stories. If three thousand were killed, there were three thousand near misses.

That day the religious died with the non-religious; Christians died alongside New Agers; Jews died with Muslims. Just as God sends sunshine and rain to the righteous and unrighteous, just so, tragedy strikes without discrimination. If we ask why one person lived while another who worked in the same office died, we cannot answer.

Yet terrorism's casualties do not increase the *ultimate* death toll. Those who did not die in New York on that fateful day would have died at a later time and in a different way. That is not to speak lightly of the horror of that day, nor does it absolve the evil men who carried out the deed. We must simply realize that death cannot be avoided because of extraordinary good health or a streak of luck. We might be able to postpone the event, but it can never be canceled altogether.

Death comes to all of us, rich and poor, famed and unsung. No matter how powerful or celebrated we may be, we cannot escape the fact of dying. It is said that the great Louis XIV of France would not allow the word *death* to be uttered in his presence. Ascending to the throne at the age of four, Louis reigned for seventy-two years, longer than any other European monarch. He built the glittering palace of Versailles. But on September 1, 1715, the "Sun King" discovered what all of us must: that death cannot be wished out of existence. When our moment comes, it will not matter whether we accepted death with tranquility, fear, or indifference; we shall find ourselves fully conscious in an eternity in which the atmosphere cannot be altered. There is literally nothing we can do about the fact that someday the bell will toll, and it will toll for us.

Which brings us to the subject of this book.

For those who believe in Him, Jesus forever changed the way we view death. Read these words carefully: "Since the children have flesh and blood, he too shared in their humanity so that by his death he might destroy him who holds the power of death—that is, the devil—and free those who all their lives were held in slavery by their fear of death" (Hebrews 2:14–15). The mission of Jesus, to put it simply, was to free us from the fear of death! Jesus came to turn an enemy into a friend, a terrifying journey into the anticipation of a welcome reunion.

How could Jesus accomplish this on our behalf? Only if He Himself became one of us, so that by His death He would destroy the fear of death that the devil used to enslave us. In other words, Satan's weapon of fear was taken from him when Jesus died and rose again. The Resurrection is proof that death need not terrify; the grave has been emptied of its power.

This is why Paul could say, "Where, O death, is your victory? Where, O death, is your sting?" (1 Corinthians 15:55). Just as a bee loses its stinger after a bite, death was emptied of its arsenal when Jesus rose from the dead. He freed us from the fear of passing through the parted curtain. Death, Paul says, has been "swallowed up in victory."

Thus the resurrection of Jesus is the cornerstone of the Christian faith. Standing at the empty tomb, we are assured of the triumph of Jesus on the Cross; we are also assured that He has conquered our most fearsome enemy. Yes, death can still terrify us, but the more we know about Jesus, the more its power fades.

For Scott and Janet Willis, heaven can't come too soon. They lost six of their nine children in a tragic van accident on November 8, 1994. Scott was driving when a metal brace fell from the truck ahead of him onto the expressway. He had no time to avoid it and could only hope that it would clear the underside of his vehicle. When the large brace reached the back of the van, the rear gas tank immediately exploded. When Scott finally had stopped the van, the inside was already engulfed in flames.

He and Janet had to put their hands into the fire to unbuckle their seat belts.

As the couple quite literally fell out of their burning vehicle, their son Benny managed to get out of the inferno, but he died later that evening. The other five children died instantly.

Scott's favorite verse of Scripture, which he quoted when standing next to the burning vehicle is Psalm 34:1, "I will bless the Lord at all times; His praise shall continually be in my mouth" (NASB). To this day the Willises affirm that God is good. What is more, they believe that their precious children died under the hand of God's providence.

"We were stewards of God's children," he says. "He gave them to us, and He took them back."

Janet explains that their sorrow is great—indescribable at times—but the sure knowledge that Christ will reunite them gives them comfort. For the Christian, death is the grand entry point into heavenly existence. Jesus has taken from us our fear of "the last enemy."

As you read these pages, you will discover that the New Testament accounts of Jesus' resurrection have answers for our questions: Why doesn't God intervene when we suffer? Is there room for doubt in the Christian life? How does Jesus view our death? What kind of body will we have a thousand years from now?

As we stand with the early disciples at the empty

tomb, we are aware that the Man who was buried there could not have been a mere mortal. Here we will discover that He triumphed where others failed; He conquered where others have been forced to confess defeat.

Standing in the presence of Jesus, we see death for what it is: a terrifying enemy whose power has been crushed. As we peer into His abandoned grave we witness death's vanishing power. Join me as we take a journey down some ancient paths that lead us to life everlasting.

CHAPTER ONE

WHEN TERROR FLED

They carry their dead as if in triumph!"

That's what the pagans observed about the Christians as plagues swept the Roman Empire. When Emperor Marcus Aurelius spoke of caravans of wagons filled with bodies making their way through the streets of Roman cities, it was the Christians who distinguished themselves from the world around them. Indeed, some historians believe that Christianity might not have become the dominant religion of Rome were it not for these massive epidemics that gave believers the opportunity to prove the triumph of the Christian faith.

If you were a pagan and a plague swept your city,

killing a third of the population, you would have to confess your ignorance regarding the meaning of such horrors. Then you would flee, trying at all costs to save your own life. When your relatives died, you would bury them without the slightest assurance that you would be reunited with them again.

But Christians accepted these tragedies differently. William McNeill writes of the Christians, "Even a shattered remnant of survivors who had somehow made it through war or pestilence or both could find warm, immediate healing and consolation in the vision of a heavenly existence for those missing relatives and friends. . . . Christianity was, therefore, a system of thought and feeling thoroughly adapted to a time of troubles in which hardship, disease, and violent death commonly prevailed."[1]

"A system of thought and feeling thoroughly adapted to a time of troubles"! Not only did the Christians accept the death of their friends with a note of triumph, but they were willing to risk their own lives to help others. Cyprian, bishop of Carthage, seems almost to have welcomed the great epidemic of his time. Writing in A.D. 251, he claimed that only non-Christians had anything to fear from the plague:

How suitable, how necessary it is that this plague and pestilence, which seems horrible and deadly, searches out the justice of each and every one and examines the minds of the human race; whether the well care for the sick, whether relatives dutifully love their kinsmen as they should, whether masters show compassion for their ailing slaves, whether physicians do not desert the afflicted. . . . Although this mortality has contributed nothing else, it has especially accomplished this for Christians and servants of God, that *we have begun gladly to seek martyrdom while we are learning not to fear death* [italics added].[2]

How should believers respond to those who have died? Cyprian continued:

Our brethren who have been freed from the world by the summons of the Lord should not be mourned, since we know that they are not lost but sent before; that in departing they lead the way; that as travelers, as voyagers are wont to be, they should be longed for, not lamented . . . and that no occasion should be given to pagans to censure us deservedly and justly, on the ground that we grieve for those who we say are living.[3]

What pagan could cease grieving, knowing that his relatives were living in heaven? Such was the confidence of the early Christians that multitudes of pagans embraced the Christian faith.

DYING WITHIN GOD'S WILL

If you think such peace in the face of death died along with the early Christians, let me give you a contemporary example of someone who faced death with the calm assurance that he was dying within the will and plan of God.

James Montgomery Boice, pastor of the historic Tenth Presbyterian Church in downtown Philadelphia, was diagnosed with inoperable cancer. Speaking to his congregation a few weeks before he died, he answered these questions for his congregation.

Should they pray for a miracle?

Well, you are free to do that, of course. My general impression is that the God who is able to do miracles —and He certainly can—is also able to keep you from getting the problem in the first place. So, although miracles happen, they are rare by definition. . . . I think it is more profitable to pray for wisdom for the doctors . . . above all, I would say pray for the glory of God. God was most glorified in the death of Jesus Christ; He did not deliver Jesus from the cross, though He could have.[4]

How should they interpret his impending death?

If I were to reflect theologically, there are two important things to remember. One is the sovereignty of God. . . . We have talked about this often. When challenges like this come into our lives, they are not accidental. It's not as if God somehow forgot what was going on and something had slipped by. . . . But it's possible to conceive that God is sovereign and yet indifferent. God's in charge, but He doesn't care. But God is not only in charge, God is also good. Everything He does is good. The will of God is pleasing and perfect. It is perfect to Him; therefore it should be perfect to us. If God does something in your life, would you change it? If you'd change it, you'd make it worse. So, that's the way we want to accept it and move forward. And who knows what God will do.[5]

Looking back, we know what God did: James Montgomery Boice died on June 15, 2000.

"ONE FORSAKEN GRAVE"

Why can Christians face death with the calm assurance that heaven awaits? The answer, of course, is because of the resurrection of Christ. The tomb that had been provided by Joseph of Arimathea was "forsaken" by Jesus of Nazareth. This fact motivated the poet Alice Meynell to write:

No planet knows that this earth of ours . . .

THE VANISHING POWER OF DEATH

Bears, as its chief treasure, one
Forsaken grave. [6]

This forsaken grave lies at the heart of the Christian faith. If Jesus did not rise, Christianity collapses like a house of cards. Vance Havner, a preacher of a past generation, said perceptively, "If the resurrection of Jesus is myth, then I am *myth*taken, *myth*stified and *myth*erable."

Why is the physical resurrection of Christ so important to our faith? First, the Resurrection fulfills Jesus' prediction that this is the final sign He would give to the world (Matthew 12:40; 16:21). Reason requires that if Christ is God, He could not stay in the tomb indefinitely.

Second, Jesus' resurrection is proof of our own final resurrection. Strictly speaking, Christ is the only person in history who was resurrected. Lazarus was simply resuscitated; he had to die again. Christ was resurrected with a new, indestructible body, a prototype of the body we shall receive. This is the hinge on which the door of Christianity swings; our faith rests on the fact of a forsaken tomb. He was raised, so we shall be also.

TRYING TO EXPLAIN THE EMPTY TOMB

Some people are unhappy about belief in the Resurrection. Hours after Jesus was buried, Pilate conspired with the chief priests and Pharisees to keep Christ in the tomb. For fear that someone might come and steal the body and claim a resurrection, Pilate gave orders: "You have a guard; go, make it as secure as you know how" (Matthew 27:65 NASB). What did Pilate have in mind when he told the leaders, "Make it as secure as you know how"? Someone has suggested that either he was laughing at the priests for their folly—imagine setting a guard to watch a dead man!—or, more likely, he was mocking them for their fears. *Do your worst! And if he is a man his body shall be kept safely in the tomb, but if he is God, he shall rise in spite of your best efforts!*

And along with a guard, they rolled that stone over the mouth of the cave to make sure it was sealed. But evidently they did not make it secure enough, for on the first day of the week the women discovered that the stone was rolled away and the tomb was empty. An angel of the Lord came from heaven and rolled back the stone and sat on it. "His appearance was like lightning, and his clothing as white as snow. The guards shook for fear of him and became like dead men" (Matthew 28:3-4 NASB). God is not intimidated by huge stones.

Alternative theories have been suggested to account for the empty tomb. Some have said that Jesus only fainted on the cross, and the cool tomb revived Him. But the Roman soldiers made sure that a man was dead before he was taken from a cross. Also, it is improbable that a wounded victim would have been able to push the heavy stone away and elude the guards. And would such a bruised, dazed Teacher be able to inspire His disciples to die for Him?

Some insist that Christ's enemies stole His body, but if that were so it would have been produced by them to stifle the disciples' preaching on the Resurrection. Against all credulity, some have speculated that the disciples themselves stole the body to fake a resurrection. But would they have been willing to die for a Christ they knew was dead?

We do well to listen to the words of J. V. Langmead Casserley in his 1951 lectures at King's College, London. He said that the attempts to explain away the empty tomb demonstrate that "the assertion of the Resurrection is like a knife pointed at the throat of the irreligious man, and an irreligious man whose religion is threatened will fight for his own creation, his most precious possession, like a tigress fighting for her cubs."[7]

FIRST-CENTURY EVIDENCE

Yet we must still answer the question: What compelling historical proof do we have that Christ has, in fact, been raised from the dead? Read again the words of the apostle Paul:

For what I received I passed on to you as of first importance: that Christ died for our sins according to the Scriptures, that he was buried, that he was raised on the third day according to the Scriptures, and that he appeared to Peter, and then to the Twelve. After that, he appeared to more than five hundred of the brothers at the same time, most of whom are still living, though some have fallen asleep. Then he appeared to James, then to all the apostles, and last of all he appeared to me also, as to one abnormally born. . . . If there is no resurrection of the dead, then not even Christ has been raised. And if Christ has not been raised, our preaching is useless and so is your faith. . . . And if Christ has not been raised, your faith is futile; you are still in your sins. (1 Corinthians 15: 3–8; 13–14, 17)

Paul is adamant in his argument: A man who claimed to be God was put to death and was raised to prove that His claims were valid. And if it were proven that the grave still contains His body, we will stop preaching and humbly admit we have been misled.

What is more, Paul says to the people in the first century, "If you don't believe that Jesus rose from the dead, just ask some of the people who saw Him after His resurrection, because many of these people are still alive! Check it out!" Here is hardheaded evidence that God invaded our world.

Perhaps you, dear reader, want to keep Christ

neatly contained in His own corner, in His tomb. But Jesus cannot be contained! He intrudes into our lives when we least expect Him. He is not put off by our attempts to keep Him at arm's length. Post your guards! Secure your stone! Make your seal! You shall confront Christ either in this life or the next.

WHAT GIVES LIFE MEANING

The Resurrection is the one fact that explains other facts and gives meaning to our lives in the midst of a decaying culture. Jesus Himself was subject to death, but in being raised with a new resurrection body, He has turned a floodlight on the center of our dingy existence. Here at last we have answers to the truly important questions of life.

First, there is no place that we must go that He has not been; He has gone before us, in death and resurrection. He does not expect us to enter a dark room that He Himself has not first entered. Our Lord goes ahead of us and promises us that we shall "see him as he is." W. Frank Harrington, the late pastor of Peachtree Presbyterian Church in Atlanta, wrote that if you study the Bible you could make the case that God is a "Go-Ahead-God." He points out that when the Israelites faced the trackless wilderness, God went before them by day in a pillar of cloud, and by night He stayed beside them with a flaming fire.

Through times of joy and suffering, through times of uncertainty and fear, God is always ahead of us. God, in fact, had gone ahead of the women rushing to the tomb, for when they arrived, the stone had already been rolled away for them. God is always going before us, to make our paths straight. And when death comes to us, as most assuredly it will, we will know that we are not traveling where Jesus has not Himself been. Death is nothing less than an encounter with God in the presence of the One who came to save us.

In fact, as believers, we shall gain by death. We shall be free from the physical and psychological trauma of this life and joined in fellowship with Jesus and our friends. Tomorrow with its heart-aches no longer need be dreaded.

Because He lives I can face tomorrow;

Because He lives all fear is gone;

Because I know He holds the future.

And life is worth the living just because He lives. [8]

Second, we who stand beside this forsaken tomb are asked to carry a message of hope to the world. The angel who was sitting within the empty tomb calmed the fears of the women and then said, "But go, tell his disciples and Peter, 'He is going ahead of you into Galilee. There you will see him, just as he told you'" (Mark 16:7).

"Tell His disciples and *Peter*." Why is Peter named? He had denied his Lord three times and felt disqualified for future usefulness and blessing. He had sworn that he didn't know Jesus after boasting that he, above all, would stay with Jesus no matter the cost. This is a message of grace to Peter, a message of grace that all of us need to hear. We speak our message to a fallen world filled with many questions and few answers. We need a message of forgiveness and reconciliation, a message of justice and eternal life. The forsaken tomb gives us the right to proclaim hope to a hopeless world.

W. Frank Harrington tells the story of a new bus driver who was not familiar with his church. It was his first Sunday, and he was in animated conversation with a woman on the bus. When he drove in, he noticed a huge cross draped in purple for the beginning of Lent. The woman said, "Right in the middle of the conversation he just forgot about me and said, 'My God, somebody big must have died!'" He was thinking about one of those little white crosses put up along the roadside when someone is killed. Well, yes, somebody big did die! And this somebody big came back to life![9]

Was Aristotle right when he said, "Death is a dreadful thing, for it is the end"? For him it meant the end of achievement, growth, companionship, love, and consciousness. Bernard Shaw said that man needs at least three hundred years to do justice to his accumulated experience and to understand his world. The poet John Keats in his early twenties was aware of his own genius but lamented, "I have fears that I may cease to be before my pen has gleaned my teeming brain."[10]

Tom Condran, a seminary classmate of mine, was diagnosed with cancer several years ago. A few weeks before he died, he called on the phone and I took notes of his final words to me. In a forced whisper he said, "These are good days. Nothing has taken away my peace and joy. When I found out that I had cancer, I feared that I would not be able to live up to the sermons I preached. But God has not allowed me to waver. The finish line is in sight. Good-bye, Erwin, I'll see you in heaven."

The forsaken tomb is an affirmation that life continues after death. God does not waste the human personality; He does not create our mind and aspirations only to have them cast aside through a stroke, heart disease, or cancer. Through Christ we have eternal life of such quality that our physical existence is but a stepping-stone to our future eternal fulfillment.

When the stone was rolled away from Christ's tomb, the terror of death fled.

CHAPTER TWO

THE FRIEND WHO CALLS OUR NAME

Many believers long to visit the Holy Land and "walk where Jesus walked." Those of us who have visited Israel have tried literally to follow in His path; we have made sure that we climbed the steps that Jesus climbed and have prayed in the garden where He prayed. We want the spirit of Jesus to grip us; we want to find Him in a special way right where He lived and taught.

Similarly, some who seek Jesus want to find Him in a statue or in the rituals of the church. But when we do this, we're looking in the wrong places. He will not be found in a specific location or among dead things! And sometimes, when we are feeling lost or lonely or grief-stricken, our tears can blind us from seeing Him. In our sorrow, we wonder where He has gone.

Just ask Mary Magdalene.

We meet Mary in a text embedded in the book of Luke, a text that reminds us that women always had a prominent role in the ministry of Jesus. "The Twelve were with him, and also some women who had been cured of evil spirits and diseases: Mary (called Magdalene) from whom seven demons had come out" (8:1–2). Other women who supported Jesus out of their own means are also listed.

Mary Magdalene was a victim; she knew the torments of alien spirits in her body. These were not just psychological scars; these were actual, personal beings that harassed her and made her unclean. We don't know how or why she acquired these foul spirits—perhaps through occultism or unrestrained immorality. Or perhaps she was a victim of abuse, and these spirits took advantage of her vulnerability.

Then she met Jesus, who told her, "Your sins are forgiven." For the first time she felt as if her spirit had been washed clean. The torment stopped; the accusing voices ended. Her friends could not account for the difference in her attitude and demeanor. The new Mary was not the woman they knew.

Recently I spoke to a distraught husband who told me that his wife would suddenly "turn into another person," venting anger for no apparent reason. This woman was tormented by some alien spirit who would bring overwhelming guilt and deep feelings of self-hate. She, like Mary, was delivered from these attacks by faith in Christ and the promise that if the Son makes us free, we are "free indeed" (John 8:36).

This was quite possibly the first time Mary met a man who did not misuse her, demean her, or manipulate her. Here was a Man of impeccable purity; a Man who could be trusted to treat her with love and respect, a Man who could forgive and accept her without degrading her with suggestive innuendoes. No wonder she was willing to contribute to His welfare with the little money she had: Those who are forgiven much love much.

LOVE TO THE END

This love motivated her to follow Him to His horrific end.

Golgotha was no place for a woman. But Mary wanted to be there, to pray, to meditate, and to grieve. In fact, we are told that she, along with Mary the mother of James and John, stayed until the very end to see where the body of Jesus was laid (Mark 15:47). The only Man who ever loved her was dead. The One who had given her her first taste of dignity, the Man who elevated her self-worth by His gracious words, was no more.

We should not be surprised that three days later we see her at the tomb. "Early on the first day of the week, while it was still dark, Mary Magdalene went to the tomb and saw that the stone had been removed from the entrance" (John 20:1). She ran to find Peter and John and to give them the sad news: "'They have taken the Lord out of the tomb, and we don't know where they have put him!'" (v. 2). She cared not to disguise the sobs. With that news, Peter and John raced toward the tomb.

John outran Peter and looked into the tomb first but did not step in. But Peter, ever brash, actually entered the tomb and saw the strips of linen and the burial cloth; then John followed him into the tomb, and we read, "He saw and believed" (v. 8). But because they still were not clear about the Resurrection, they simply left the area and returned to their homes.

But Mary Magdalene refused to leave.

This woman, bless her, would not be put off; she would try to find the body, or at least find where it was to be found. She loved this Man who had set her free; she wanted to honor the memory of a man she could trust. This woman was on a mission to make sure she knew where His body was and that it had been properly cared for.

She stood beside the tomb, crying. "As she wept, she bent over to look into the tomb and saw two angels in white, seated where Jesus' body had been, one at the head, the other at the foot. They asked her, 'Woman, why are you crying?'

"'They have taken my Lord away,' she said, 'and I don't know where they have put him'" (John 20:11–13).

We might be surprised at her seemingly calm response to these divine messengers. Keep in mind that in those days people were accustomed to miracles, especially because of the works of Jesus and the prevailing belief that angelic visitors did in fact occasionally bring messages from heaven. Also, Mary was so preoccupied with her grief that she probably did not care about the identity of these messengers. Her loss was too great to be concerned with formal introductions.

Mary did not want angels; she wanted her Lord. In those days, like today, some people believed that angels are more accessible than God; but Mary cared not for their company. She longed only for Jesus, and if she could not have Him alive, at least she could honor His decaying body.

Has anyone ever *loved* like this woman?

Has anyone ever *wept* like this woman?

Has anyone ever *cared* like this woman?

She peered into the dark tomb long enough to be satisfied that it was empty. She was contemplating what to do next. Slowly she backed away and straightened herself, her eyes adjusting to the light around her.

THE UNEXPECTED MEETING

"At this, she turned around and saw Jesus standing there, but she did not realize that it was Jesus.

" 'Woman,' he said, 'why are you crying? Who is it you are looking for?' Thinking he was the gardener, she said, 'Sir, if you have carried him away, tell me where you have put him, and I will get him'" (vv. 14–15).

"Tell Me Where You Have Put Him."

She does not know that she is in the presence of the One whom she seeks. Grief—deep grief—can blur reality for us. In our dark moments we cannot see Christ even when He stands beside us.

Why did she not recognize Jesus?

She was looking in *the wrong place.* She was looking for a corpse, not the living Lord. She was "seeking the living among the dead" (see Luke 24:5). She thought that her last act of appreciation would be to care for His dead body. Her hopes rose no higher than to find a corpse.

How sad if Mary had found what she was looking for! What a tragedy if her Master's lifeless body had simply been carried to another tomb! Pity her if she had found a body that needed her care. Thankfully, God sometimes does not let us find what we are looking for.

Mary was also looking in the *wrong direction*. When she was peering into the tomb, she had her back to Him. She must not look *into* the tomb but *out* of it; she must not look for a dead Christ but a living one. She was looking for Him in a place where He does not belong.

Bunyan in *The Pilgrim's Progress* tells us about a Christian who would always keep his eyes riveted on the floor and failed to look up. For him, life was but an experience of this world, not the world to come. As long as we are looking down, we cannot look up to our Father in heaven. The direction we face determines what we will discover and the destination we shall reach.

The gardener asked her a question, and she turned to reply to this stranger whom she presumed might be able to help her. Think again about her words: "Sir, if you have carried Him away, tell me where you have laid Him and I will take Him away" (John 20:15 NASB). She did not know that she was speaking to her Lord.

Nor could she have known what she had just said. Even if Jesus had been of slight weight, Mary could hardly have thought that she would be able to carry His body with the heavy ointments wrapped in the linen cloths. But as Donald Grey Barnhouse wrote, "Here is one of the greatest character portrayals of all of literature, human or divine. Here is the heart of a good woman. Here is love, offering to do the impossible as love always does."[1] Jesus no doubt was touched by her devotion.

"Mary."

Now Jesus looks into her eyes and says but one word, *"Mary."*

The voice, the presence . . .a second look, and *yes,* it is Jesus! No one ever said her name just like that!

In a flash she responds, "'Rabboni!' (which means Teacher)" (v. 16). She falls at His feet, clinging to Him, determined to not let go.

Mary will leave the garden a different woman. Her sorrow has vanished as thoroughly as the darkness in a sun-drenched room. Her grief is a memory, a reminder of her failure to recognize her Master standing at her side. Her Beloved who was dead is now alive and knows her by name. Nothing important has changed, yet everything is different.

What a Friend We Have . . .

And He called her by name.

"Mary!" He said.

The name *Mary* is a compound of two Hebrew words, which means "exalted by the Lord." The Lord exalted her by giving her the privilege of being the first person to whom He revealed Himself. She sees Jesus before Peter, James, or John does. Imagine the honor of experiencing this first revelation of the living Jesus!

"Your Master Is Here."

He speaks her name tenderly, for the Lord does not call her "Mary Magdalene," as a reminder of her past life, but just "Mary," the name of personal identification and compassion. Jesus knows her tears, her sorrows, her hopelessness. "Dry your tears, Mary. Behold, your Master is here, and He is calling you."

Earlier in His ministry Jesus said, "My sheep listen to my voice; I know them, and they follow me. I give them eternal life, and they shall never perish; no one can snatch them out of my hand" (John 10:27–28). Mary was one of His sheep and He called her by name, and she knew His voice. And she was willing to follow Him to death.

One of the sweetest words we can hear is our own name. That single word *Mary* changed everything for this grieving woman. This word proved that Jesus was alive for her and for anyone else who desires His companionship. She had hoped for a dead Christ, but now the living Christ was calling her.

Jesus was fulfilling the promise of Isaiah 61:3, providing "beauty instead of ashes [and] . . . gladness instead of mourning." One word, and death,

Satan, and hell are conquered. One word, and loneliness and fear vanish. One word, and Mary knows she will never have to feel hopeless again. The encounter was up close and personal.

A Learning Experience

For Mary, this was also a learning experience. When she clasped His feet, Jesus said to her, "Do not hold on to me, for I have not yet returned to the Father. Go instead to my brothers and tell them, 'I am returning to my Father and your Father, to my God and your God'" (John 20:17). She clung to His feet like a child who fears the departure of a parent. Now that she had found Him, she did not want to lose Him.

There was nothing wrong with Mary's clinging to Jesus; most assuredly, He could be touched, for later He challenged His disciples, "Touch me and see; a ghost does not have flesh and bones" (Luke 24:39). Thomas was invited to touch His nail prints.

But for now, Jesus said, "Don't do that."

He was in effect saying, "You will see Me again, for I have not yet ascended to My Father. Don't think you will lose Me, because I will be with you for the next forty days. No need to panic." Yes, it was the same Jesus, but the nature of the relationship would change.

After the Ascension Jesus was taken to heaven

and then returned in the person of the Holy Spirit so that He now indwells all of His people simultaneously. He is as much with us as He was with Mary. We, like her, have to understand that Christ's presence is not dependent on the location of His physical body. She had to be weaned from the notion that physical contact superseded the spiritual connection.

For now, Mary had a job to do; she had to tell the disciples that the Lord was alive. She could not selfishly keep her arms around Jesus, as though He belonged only to her. So she left and found the disciples to tell them that she had seen the Lord. Imagine, a formerly demon-possessed woman is the first to tell the good news to others!

An Affirming Experience

Finally, it was an experience of affirmation. Let's revisit the words, "I ascend to My Father and your Father, and My God and your God" (John 20:17 NASB). What is Jesus saying to this woman whose past was steeped in sin and mental distress?

With this comment, He introduces Mary to the deepest level of acceptance and fellowship! Consider: Early in His ministry, Jesus called the disciples His servants; that surely was an honor of unimaginable significance. But in the Upper Room He became more intimate: "I no longer call you servants, because a servant does not know his master's business. Instead, I have called you friends, for everything that I learned from my Father I have made known to you" (John 15:15). From servants to friends—a giant step in closeness and importance.

Now, in the presence of Mary, He reveals an even deeper level of intimacy. In affirming that He and Mary had the same Father, He was saying that they were Brother and sister! Servants, yes; friends, yes; now, brothers and sisters within the same family! What an honor for a woman who had at one time fallen under the spell of evil spirits!

A text that I've had to dare myself to believe is found in Hebrews 2. Please read it as if you have never seen it before.

> In bringing many sons to glory, it was fitting that God, for whom and through whom everything exists, should make the author of their salvation perfect through suffering. Both the one who makes men holy and those who are made holy are of the same family. So Jesus is not ashamed to call them brothers. He says, "I will declare your name to my brothers; in the presence of the congregation I will sing your praises." (vv. 10–12)

We are His brothers and sisters, and He is not ashamed to say so! Mary had to learn that she was not just Jesus' friend—but His sister.

When John was with Jesus at the table, he leaned

against His bosom; but years later when he saw the resurrected Christ on the Island of Patmos he wrote, "I fell at his feet as though dead" (Revelation 1:17). Jesus is at once Brother and Lord; Companion and Judge.

Today Mary lives on the pages of the New Testament to give hope to all who struggle with self-hatred; hope for those who struggle with demons, whether real or imagined. Standing at the empty tomb, we too can turn from our despair to the One who proved that death does not have the final word.

NOT ALONE AFTER ALL

In those moments when we feel betrayed by friends or by life itself, we must remember that Christ's presence is not dependent on our perception of Him. He is among us even when we cannot see Him and when our grief distorts reality. There are many tears in our hearts that never reach our eyes. There are times of darkness and betrayal that make us wonder how we can live another day. As for God, He seems far away, uninterested, and absent.

We've all had moments when we were in an emotional free fall, without hope of finding solid ground beneath our feet. News that we have a terminal disease, the death of a marriage partner, or the crime of a wayward child can throw us into despair. Trials can undermine what we have always believed about God, prayer, and the church.

But these moments, dark as they are, cannot compare to the loss of God in our lives, that feeling that He is not there for us when we need Him the most. Think of what it would be like, not just to lose a friend or a spouse, but to lose fellowship with God. Imagine living with His absence, convinced that His promises had fallen to the ground.

When He Calls Our Name

Then think of how in a moment of time, all is changed when we hear Him call our name. Like Mary, our despair is replaced with the certainty that we have not been forgotten. If we have her heart, we shall hear His voice. Today He calls us, whether our name is Ted, Ruth, or Peter. Jesus calls, if only we were to listen.

And there at the empty tomb, we are reminded that Jesus is beside us to give us the wisdom and the comfort we seek. We are not alone after all.

In our distress, we can look into the tomb and see glory. I remember talking to a man who described how difficult it was for him to choose a cemetery plot. Just the knowledge that his relatives would come to that very spot to visit his grave made him dread the assignment. Somehow, standing there amid the tombstones, he was forced to contemplate his own mortality.

The empty tomb of Jesus assures us that we need not fear when our own tomb is finally put to use. Because His tomb is empty, we need not fear when ours is full. With Mary we can say, "I have seen the Lord!" Our Beloved also calls our name and reminds us that we matter.

When my wife and I were newlyweds, we were taken to dinner by an older couple who pointed out their cemetery plots as we drove past the graveyard. "Do you think the Lord will remember our names and where we will be buried?" the wife asked, almost to herself, as if she was not expecting an answer. The story of Mary reminds us that yes, He will remember, and, yes, He will call us by name on the final day of resurrection. We do not hear the voice of an earthly gardener, but the Lord, the Keeper of our hearts.

When Knights and Kings Die

In Marburg, Germany, there is a sarcophagus with two layers. On the top, a Teutonic knight is dressed in splendor, a compelling reminder of his power and pomp. Then beneath we see the jarring contrast of a decaying corpse overrun by snakes and toads.

The two representations illustrate the vanity of

life. At the present time we may savor wealth, recognition, and the enjoyment of the finer things of life. But if we wait a while, we will pass away, and what matters now will not matter then. First the riches, then the rot; first the glory, then the clay.

A priest took a king to a room filled with skeletons and said, "Here, among the corpses of slaves, lies a king." He had made his point: In death a king is indistinguishable from a servant. "No matter how high the glory, there's always the same end to the story, decay and rot."[2]

Yet, despite the rot on earth, we can contemplate the triumph of heaven. Instead of mud we have marble, and in the place of gloom there is glory. "Jesus lives and so shall I," we sing. His victory in His tomb translates into victory in ours. No place, no disciple, no gardener can substitute for Him. Only when He calls our name are we satisfied.

Back in the late 1800s, Jennie Evelyn Hussey spent much of her time taking care of her invalid sister. She never complained but accepted it as "from the Lord." Later, when she was almost paralyzed by deformative arthritis, she prayed that she would be able to carry her cross without complaint, just as Jesus had borne His. Her experience became the inspiration for the hymn "Lead Me to Calvary." The third stanza reads:

Let me like Mary, through the gloom,
Come with a gift to Thee;
Show to me now the empty tomb,
Lead me to Calvary. [3]

The Lord who called "Mary!" called Jennie Hussey and all who will put their trust in Him. We, like they, can prove our devotion in the presence of the One who stood with Mary beside His empty tomb. Jesus always stands in the presence of those who believe.

HOW JESUS RESURRECTS OUR DREAMS

When I was a professor at Moody Bible Institute, my secretary, a young woman of twenty-one, was diagnosed with a very rare form of cancer. But our hopes rose with a new drug that seemingly worked a miracle. Many of us picked up on her optimism, believing and praying that she had overcome the disease. But, a few months later, she died. At her funeral I remember thinking, *Why did God raise our hopes only to have them dashed to pieces?* Better to not have believed than to believe and receive no for an answer.

Disease can shatter our dreams and jolt our trust in God. As I write, we've been assured that SARS (sudden acute respiratory syndrome) is under control, but AIDS is making a silent but powerful comeback. No cure has been found for cancer or heart disease. Walk through a hospital, and you will soon confront many shattered dreams.

The debris of shattered dreams lies everywhere, even on a roadside. Seventeen-year-old twins in southern Illinois were driving to school when their car careened off the highway and hit a tree. One of the boys was killed instantly; the other, named Steven, is struggling to recover. Many dreams died that day in a speeding car.

Disappointment—the sense of being let down by life and, indeed, by God—leaves many dreams destroyed in its wake. A mother said, "Long ago I've given up on God and I've given up on prayer. I prayed to God and asked that my daughter would become a missionary. She not only is not a missionary, but she's married to an unconverted man. I'm never going to bother God with another request again, because it hurts when you're disappointed by Him."

And if we have not felt betrayed by God, we most assuredly have felt betrayed by others—often those we have considered our friends. Some have had to cope with abuse, anger, and manipulation. We have the highest hopes for enjoying fulfilling relationships, but often our best efforts fail. Dreams aplenty lie shattered at our feet.

Behind these disappointments lies the painful knowledge that things would have been different—

if God had only intervened. If you were to ask skeptics why they disbelieve, they would readily speak of their bitter disappointment with the Almighty. After all, if He is omnipotent, if He can do whatever He wishes whenever He wishes, why does He not take charge and make wrong things right? Why all these shattered dreams? Why these unfulfilled longings? What good is omnipotence if it is not used to make a crooked world straight?

Two Disappointed Disciples

Let's follow the story of two disciples who were deeply disappointed by Jesus. On the first day of the week, three days after Jesus had been crucified, some women had gone to His tomb and reported that He was alive. But many thought their testimony was suspect; after all, one of the witnesses was Mary Magdalene, whom we met in the previous chapter. She had been possessed by seven demons—was her story about seeing the Lord prompted by an eighth? Some of the disciples went to the tomb and agreed that it was empty, but Jesus they did not see.

So two disciples set out to walk away from Jerusalem to the little town of Emmaus about seven miles distant. They hoped to get away from the commotion and the sadness of the past three days. "Now that same day two of them were going to a village called Emmaus, about seven miles from

Jerusalem. They were talking with each other about everything that had happened" (Luke 24:13–14).

A stranger falls in step with them—it is Jesus, but they don't recognize Him. He asked, "What are you discussing together as you walk along?" We read: "They stood still, their faces downcast. One of them, named Cleopas, asked him, 'Are you only a visitor to Jerusalem and do not know the things that have happened there in these days?'"

"'What things?' he asked." (Of course, Jesus knew exactly what they had been talking about. He wanted to hear what the two would say.)

"'About Jesus of Nazareth,' they replied. 'He was a prophet, powerful in word and deed before God and all the people. The chief priests and our rulers handed him over to be sentenced to death, and they crucified him; but we had hoped that he was the one who was going to redeem Israel. And what is more, it is the third day since all this took place. In addition, some of our women amazed us. They went to the tomb early this morning but didn't find his body. They came and told us that they had seen a vision of angels, who said he was alive. Then some of our companions went to the tomb and found it just as the women had said, but him they did not see'" (vv. 17–24).

You can hear the pathos behind the words: "We had hoped . . . "

We thought He was the Messiah! We pinned our

hopes on Him! the two followers were implying. *We dreamed that He was going to redeem Israel; we thought He would bring political redemption by defeating the Romans, restoring Jewish rule, and putting an end to injustice. We thought this would be the end of the hated Roman tax collectors and the humiliating occupation by these pagan foreigners.* He had the marks of a redeemer, yet seemingly He did not redeem.

Truth be told, the disappointment of these two disciples was deeper than the fact that Jesus failed to live up to expectations. They felt betrayed by Someone they loved. Yes, they pinned their messianic hopes on Him, but they also had given Him their devotion, their loyalty. The hurt ran deep because their love ran deep. He gave them a dream and did not deliver.

Keep in mind that these disciples were probably on hand when Jesus took the lunch and fed a multitude of five thousand people; they knew He could walk on water and cause the deaf to hear and the lame to walk. He had all the power of the Messiah, but when the Romans came to arrest Him, He didn't use it. He went meekly off to His death as if He were as helpless as an ordinary man. They had hoped for better than that.

The bystanders at the cross reported on the tragic end of a beautiful life. With His wrenching death, all hopes were lost. These disciples thought they would never smile again. They'd come through an emotional earthquake, and they did not see how there could be a happy end to their story. Exhausted, they preferred to forget it all.

DIVINE ANSWERS TO DISAPPOINTMENTS

Jesus would help them overcome their disappointments. Far from being betrayed by Him, they would learn that He was as good as His word. Rather than being a disappointment, Jesus would fulfill their wildest and most ambitious dreams.

What this stranger—Jesus—did for them, He will do for us. He takes no dreams from us He does not return; He raises no hopes He does not fulfill; He gives us no longings that shall not be satisfied. The answer He gave these discouraged disciples becomes our answer too.

As Jesus walked with them, He acted in His role as Counselor. Here we get a glimpse of what it would be like if Jesus were to walk with us through our depression, discouragement, and unfulfilled aspirations. We see tenderness, rebuke, and instruction. Best of all, we see that our perspectives are challenged and changed in His presence.

SUFFERING AND GLORY

What should we do when our world comes apart? What do we do with the dreams that lie shattered at our feet? What do we do when everything we have believed about God seems destroyed? Jesus pointed these two disciples back to the Scriptures and said that an answer can be found there, if only they were listening!

We are invited to eavesdrop.

"He said to them, 'How foolish you are, and how slow of heart to believe all that the prophets have spoken! Did not the Christ have to suffer these things and then enter his glory?' And beginning with Moses and all the Prophets, he explained to them what was said in all the Scriptures concerning himself" (vv. 25–27).

They knew the Bible, didn't they? Yes, they knew its basic teachings, but they had the twin problems of forgetfulness and confusion. So Jesus began with the Bible's story line to help them understand why recent events in Jerusalem should make sense to them.

Perhaps He began with Genesis 3:15, explaining how the seed of the woman would crush the head of the serpent. Then He might have gone to Genesis 22, where Abraham was about to offer Isaac but God provided a ram caught in the thicket, which represented the substitute "Lamb of God." Then He may have reminded them of Exodus 12 and said, "Didn't you understand that the blood of lambs on the doorpost of the Israelites in Egypt that shielded them from God's wrath—didn't you understand the sacrifice was a picture of Messiah?"

Next Jesus might have gone to the Psalms to point out that the words "My God, my God, why have you forsaken me?" (Psalm 22:1) were a reference to the Messiah dying on a cross for the sins of the world. Then perhaps to Isaiah 53, which says of Him, "But he was pierced for our transgressions, he was crushed for our iniquities; the punishment that brought us peace was upon him, and by his wounds we are healed. We all, like sheep, have gone astray, each of us has turned to his own way; and the LORD has laid on him the iniquity of us all" (vv. 5–6). This is Messiah as a Lamb led off to the slaughter.

Suffering Precedes Glory

How could this discussion have revived the shattered hopes of disciples who were disappointed with Jesus? Jesus is saying that they should have known that Messiah had to suffer first before He could enter into His glory. First the suffering, then the glory; first the cross, then the crown; first the pain, then the gain. When Jesus was hauled away to be crucified, God's plan was on target.

Remember that the people were not wrong in thinking that the Messiah would set things right on earth, but they were wrong regarding the timetable. Today, we have health-and-wealth preachers who tell us that our bodies can be healed, that we can live with luxury, and that we should always be able to enjoy life—and they are right, but wrong about the time frame. In this life, we have suffering; in the next, blessings that the most eloquent orator cannot describe. "In this world you will have trouble," Jesus once told His disciples. "But take heart! I have overcome the world" (John 16:33*b*).

Today not everyone is going to be healed. Nor are we promised wealth if we send a seed gift to a televangelist. The Bible does not promise that we will be shielded from injustices, loneliness, and persecution. In fact, Jesus said, "If they persecuted me, they will persecute you also" (John 15:20). We should expect no more than Jesus got when He was on earth. Paul says we must through much suffering enter into the kingdom of heaven (see Acts 14:22).

Suffering does not reflect unfavorably on the promises of Scripture. We take heart that there is another world coming, in which all of the promised blessings will be realized. Just as God does not create a single fish without creating water in which it can swim, so God does not create longings for eternity without creating an eternity in which those longings will be fulfilled.

Suffering Intensifies Our Desire for Glory

Suffering not only precedes glory, but suffering intensifies our desire for glory. Here at Moody Church, we have adopted a refugee camp in southern Africa, so we have teams that visit there several times a year. We have helped them build a church and have sent many containers of clothes and food supplements. I'm told that those people speak often of heaven and long for the day when they will arrive where there is no hunger and thirst—and where the Lord Himself is present. Heaven seems remote in affluent cultures, but it is ever present on the minds of those who suffer. First comes Good Friday, then Resurrection Sunday.

Of course I'm not saying that God offers us nothing on earth; to the contrary, life as a Christian is more fulfilling than anything we could find among the shallow values of the world. But we only taste the blessings now; we will enjoy them in abundance in the life to come. We have the drop but await the ocean; we have the flower, but we shall enjoy the garden.

What these discouraged disciples lacked was the proper time line. Jesus chided them that if they had understood the Scriptures they could have spared themselves the despair and loss they carried in their souls.

Our despair, like theirs, begins to vanish when

we understand and believe the Scriptures. And yet our souls long for something else. The bare words of Scripture must be believed, but we crave the divine presence. So we move on to find out what happened when this trio reached Emmaus.

HIS PERSONAL PRESENCE

The seven-mile walk ends. "As they approached the village to which they were going, Jesus acted as if he were going farther" (Luke 24:28). Jesus does not impose Himself on their privacy and schedules. He did not want them to feel an obligation to invite Him over for an evening meal. "But they urged him strongly, 'Stay with us, for it is nearly evening; the day is almost over.' So he went in to stay with them" (v. 29).

This stranger intrigues them, although they still don't recognize Him. They knew He was special, for He opened the Scriptures as no one had. There was kindness in His voice—along with sadness that they had been so slow to understand the Bible's story line. No wonder they urged Him to stay with them.

They're enjoying Middle East hospitality when suddenly their guest becomes the host. "When he was at the table with them, he took bread, gave thanks, broke it and began to give it to them" (v. 30). He was invited to receive, but once welcomed, He comes to give and to bless. "Then their eyes were opened and they recognized him, and he disappeared from their sight" (v. 31).

Of course, liberal scholars have ridiculed the idea that Jesus just vanished into "thin air." They can't bring themselves to believe in a vanishing Jesus, because they don't believe in a *divine* Jesus. But for those who believe that Jesus is who He claimed to be, it is not difficult to believe that His resurrection body was capable of disappearing and returning to Jerusalem in a moment of time.

Dumbfounded Disciples

The two disciples are dumbfounded, chiding themselves for not recognizing their divine guest. They reminisce about the events of the afternoon. "Were not our hearts burning within us while he talked with us on the road and opened the Scriptures to us?" (v. 32). And they rose that very hour and returned to Jerusalem—all seven miles—and they found the eleven closest disciples gathered together along with some friends, and they were all saying, "It is true! The Lord has risen and has appeared to Simon" (v. 34). Then the two who had been to Emmaus and back added their story, telling about how He walked with them and was recognized by them in the breaking of bread.

They had one more surprise before bedtime.

The group had not yet dispersed, and we read, "While they were still talking about this, Jesus himself stood among them and said to them, 'Peace be with you'" (v. 36). The Crucifixion was then; the Resurrection is now.

To understand the Scriptures was wonderful, but to have the risen Jesus standing among them was more glorious than they could have imagined. Now they did not only simply believe the bare words of the prophets, they were experiencing the personal presence of the One whom they loved.

With Us When We Do Not See Him

Why did Jesus appear to the disciples and then vanish? He wanted them to know that He was just as much with them when they didn't see Him as He was when He was breaking bread at their table. Lest we envy the disciples who actually saw the physical form of Jesus, we must keep in mind that this same Jesus is with us too; we must think of Him as standing at our side, riding with us in the car, and walking with us into our apartment. We don't have to see Him for us to know that He is there. And best of all, He will stay at our side, guiding us all the way to our heavenly home.

"But I tell you the truth," Jesus told them just days earlier. "It is for your good that I am going away. Unless I go away, the Counselor will not come to you; but if I go, I will send him to you" (John 16:7). After the Ascension, Jesus sent the Holy Spirit to indwell believers all over the world and to give the assurance of His presence to all who belong to Him. Rather than being limited to one place at one time, He is now with us simultaneously by the presence of His Spirit.

They thought that death would silence Him,
They nailed Him to a tree;
But I am sure He rose again
Because He lives in me.
I never envy those who heard Him
Preach in Galilee;
For since my heart has turned to Him
He daily walks with me.
I never wish that I had walked
With Him beside the Galilean Sea;
For here and now on Atlanta streets,
He often walks with me.
They thought that death would conquer Him;
They nailed Him to a tree.
I know. I know He conquered death,
Because He lives in me.[1]

The companionship of Jesus gives us courage. Though there might have been dangers late at night, nothing could keep the two disciples from Emmaus from returning to Jerusalem to tell their friends the news. They knew that they were not walking back alone; though invisible, Jesus was just as much with them in the darkness of night as He was in the sunlight at noon. Jesus walked with them in both directions along the Emmaus road.

How does Christ revive our shattered dreams? How does He come to us in our gloom and give us a reason to live and a reason to hope?

No Wasted Sorrows

As we walk along our own private journey to Emmaus, the resurrected Jesus walks with us. Thanks to His triumph, we know that we are never forsaken. He understands our hopes and dreams and knows the depths of our pain and disappointment. He is there to point us back to the Scriptures and remind us that we are not alone. He picks up the pieces of our shattered dreams and gives us a reason to go on.

Years ago, I visited the redwood forest of California. There I discovered that trees blown over in a windstorm lie dormant in the brush, but years later, a new tree grows from their roots. In fact, the new trees use the broken ones as a part of their root system. Out of the failure, new and stronger trees arise.

Every shattered dream we give to Jesus is integrated into a higher and even more blessed purpose. In short, if we have faith to believe it, there are no wasted sorrows, no wasted aspirations or dreams. Even in this life, we see that God is continually reshaping whatever we give Him. Indeed, the Christian life is a series of new beginnings. God Himself rushes in to fill the vacuum left in the wake of our own disappointments.

Dreams left unfulfilled in this life will most assuredly be fulfilled in the life to come. Jesus brought our dream of healthy bodies back with Him when He was raised from the dead. Take a long look at the person sitting next to you in church. Someday he or she will be like Jesus! "Because I live, you also will live" (John 14:19).

To those who are brokenhearted, Jesus assures us that fulfilling family relationships will be ours. As we learned in Jesus' encounter with Mary, He says, "I am your Brother; I am your Father; I am your Friend." The fulfillment of our deepest desires for friendship and acceptance awaits us. Even our longing for security and wealth will be fully realized. We are, after all, "heirs of God and co-heirs with Christ" (Romans 8:17). And "he who overcomes will inherit these things" (Revelation 21:7 NASB). We do not have to win in this life in order to win in the next.

A doctor, not thinking that a dying girl could hear him, said to her mother, "Poor child, she has seen her best days." But she was listening and was able to whisper, "No, my best days are still to come." Our problem, simply put, is that like the disciples, we do not recognize Jesus as He walks with us. We fail to see Him in the circumstances He brings into our lives; we fail to see Him in our hardships and disappointments. He is here, but our eyes are clouded with our own faithlessness and failures. Blessed are those who see Jesus when others see Him not.

A friend of mine told me of the sadness he felt when his mother was discovered dead in her apartment several days after her death. "To think that she died alone," he said. But his mother was a believer in Jesus, so I assured him, "She did not die alone. The resurrected Jesus was with her on both sides of the parted curtain."

Jesus would have kept going past the disciples' home if they had not urged Him to stay. Just so, He will pass by the door of our lives if, in our indifference, we fail to recognize His presence. "Here I am! I stand at the door and knock. If anyone hears my voice and opens the door, I will come in and eat with him, and he with me" (Revelation 3:20). This is an invitation for believers to open the door of their lives and invite Jesus to be their sacred and very personal guest.

Back in 1932, a pastor in California was shaving one Sunday morning when he heard a religiously liberal minister on the radio say, "Good morning, it is Easter." Then the radio preacher went on to say that it really did not matter whether Christ was risen or not; as far as he was concerned, Christ's body could be dust. What mattered is that the "truth" and "inspiration" of the Resurrection would continue with us.

Pastor Alfred Ackley then shouted at the radio, loudly enough for his wife to hear, "It's a lie!" That Sunday Ackley preached on the truth of the Resurrection more fervently than he had in the past. He even preached on the Resurrection that Sunday evening!

His wife suggested that he work out his frustration by writing a song that would live beyond him. That evening he wrote the words of a hymn and composed the tune on the piano.

I serve a risen Savior, He's in the world today;
I know that He is living, whatever men may say;
I see His hand of mercy, I hear His voice of cheer,
And just the time I need Him He's always near.
He lives, He lives, Christ Jesus lives today!
He walks with me and talks with me along life's
    narrow way.

He lives, He lives, salvation to impart!

You ask me how I know He lives?

He lives within my heart. [2]

For those who are willing to believe, the risen Christ is with us to guide, to give assurance, and to fellowship with us. In His presence our broken dreams are redirected to serve His higher purposes. In His eternal presence, all God-given dreams will eventually come to pass.

C H A P T E R   F O U R

CAN YOU BELIEVE AND STILL DOUBT?

When Larry Crabb, a Christian counselor, was but fifteen years old, his father offered the assurance of salvation to his comatose father-in-law. On the way out of the hospital, Mr. Crabb told his wife, "Soon your dad will be with the Lord . . . if it's all true."

Young Larry ran up to his father and asked, "What do you mean, 'if'?"

"Well, I don't know," he replied. "Sometimes I wonder."

Can we believe and still add an *if?*

Ours is an age of skepticism. Politicians make promises they do not intend to keep. Clergymen are accused of sexual abuse, cover-ups, and worse.

Corporate executives have betrayed their clients while they themselves live in luxury. Recently the truth came out about a seemingly upright, well-known Christian leader who betrayed his wife for the past eleven years. His wife now says, "I can't trust anyone . . . I'm beginning to think that everyone is suspect." Surrounded by such examples of lies and broken trust, it's not surprising many of us find it hard *not* to doubt most people and their promises!

Even when we are faced with the unassailable truths of Scripture, we can wonder, like Larry Crabb's dad: *Is it really all true?* Even when we have followed Christ for a lifetime, we can wrestle with skepticism: *Did it really happen like that?*

Well, is there room for doubt in the Christian life? I think the answer is yes, for sometimes doubt is really the raw side of honesty. By *doubt,* I do not mean *unbelief;* they appear to be the same, but there are differences. Unbelief has been defined as rebellion against evidence that we cannot or will not accept. But doubt is simply stumbling over a stone that we do not yet understand. Unbelief—especially the hardened variety—is kicking at a stone that we understand all too well.

A dishonest doubter always raises the bar. Often he wants evidence that is not available—like the man who once said to me, "I'd believe in God if He came out of heaven and spoke to me." Or like the agnostic college girl who prayed, "God, I don't believe You exist, but if You're there, prove it by making me beautiful by morning." Those who pray such prayers will never overcome their doubts.

AN HONEST DOUBTER

You see, there's a difference between honest doubt and dishonest doubt. By honest doubt, I mean an attitude of openness to the evidence. An honest doubter is willing to change his mind—if the data warrants it.

Enter "Doubting Thomas."

When we meet Thomas in heaven, I wonder if he is going to be glad about the "Doubting" that is invariably attached to his name. He was a doubter, but thankfully he was an honest doubter; and when the evidence was presented to him, he became a fervent believer.

The Loyal Pessimist

What do we know about him?

Someone has described Thomas as a "loyal pessimist," someone who saw the cup half empty rather than half full. When Jesus said He was going to Jerusalem to die, Thomas said, "Let us also go, that we may die with him" (John 11:16). He had that melancholy attitude, believing that if Jesus died, he, along with all the other disciples, would join the death march. Yet we can't help but admire his loyalty: He did not shrink from a willingness to suffer for his Master.

We get another glimpse of him in John 14. Jesus tells the disciples that He is going away to the Father, and then adds, "You know the way to the place where I am going" (v. 4). Thomas speaks on behalf of the other disciples: "Lord, we don't know where you are going, so how can we know the way?" (v. 5). In effect, he's saying, "Lord, I don't get all this metaphysical stuff about You going somewhere and we know where You're going. Just tell us." We're all glad when someone asks the question that is on our own minds.

We can be glad for Thomas's question, for it prompted Jesus to make one of His most memorable "I Am" claims. "I am the way and the truth and the life. No one comes to the Father except through me" (John 14:6).

A Tragedy with No Happy Ending?

But the best-known story of Thomas is when he doubted the resurrection of Jesus. As far as he was concerned, the Crucifixion was the end of the Master he had come to love. All that Thomas could think about was blood, scars, nails, and an angry mob. He, like most of the other disciples, ran to hide when

Jesus was crucified. Like the disciples en route to Emmaus, Thomas was convinced that this was one tragedy that could not have a happy ending.

The disciples were convinced that the tomb was empty, but that meant little since Jesus was nowhere to be found. They met together to console themselves and to process the stories and rumors that were circulating in Jerusalem. Once inside their favorite meeting room, they kept the doors locked for fear of being arrested. Then we read these startling words:

> *On the evening of that first day of the week, when the disciples were together, with the doors locked for fear of the Jews, Jesus came and stood among them and said, "Peace be with you!" After he said this, he showed them his hands and side. The disciples were overjoyed when they saw the Lord. Again Jesus said, "Peace be with you! As the Father has sent me, I am sending you." And with that he breathed on them and said, "Receive the Holy Spirit. If you forgive anyone his sins, they are forgiven; if you do not forgive them, they are not forgiven." (John 20:19–23)*

Perhaps because of his melancholy disposition, Thomas was absent, preferring to brood by himself. Angry people like to be left alone; so do those who are hurt or those filled with self-pity. Whatever the reason, Thomas missed a very important Sunday evening service!

When the disciples met up with him, they were exuberant. "We have seen the Lord!" they shouted with one voice. We might expect Thomas to rejoice too: Sure, he missed the meeting, but at least Jesus was known to be alive! An attorney would be delighted with this kind of evidence—ten men, all saying the same thing, telling the same story, spontaneously and with enthusiasm. But it wasn't enough for Thomas.

GLIMMERS AMID DARKNESS

Should he have believed in the Resurrection whether or not he saw Jesus? Thomas's faith should have been strengthened by remembering the predictions of Jesus Himself. "A wicked and adulterous generation asks for a miraculous sign! But none will be given it except the sign of the prophet Jonah. For as Jonah was three days and three nights in the belly of a huge fish, so the Son of Man will be three days and three nights in the heart of the earth" (Matthew 12:39–40). Even more explicitly, Jesus later told the disciples that He must go to Jerusalem to suffer and die and that "on the third day [He would] be raised to life" (Matthew 16:21).

. . . for a Hurting Disciple

Thomas should have put the two together: the

promises of Jesus and the recent testimony of his friends. But he was hurting, so he nourished his skepticism. Though he had every reason to believe, he steadfastly maintained his "wait-and-see" attitude. If he was going to believe, he needed more evidence. The bare prediction of Jesus was not enough.

Don't you envy people who have a very simple faith? I know a man who just believes and trusts. He does not seem to be bothered trying to reconcile the love of God with the Holocaust or child abuse. Somehow, questions that trouble many of us never bother him. But for some of us, faith comes harder.

. . . for a Blind Pastor

In 1842 George Matheson was born in Glasgow, Scotland. Later, although he was a blind college student, his sisters helped him earn two degrees at the University of Glasgow. As a minister he memorized his sermons, along with the Scripture and the hymns for each of the services. Obviously, he knew the Scriptures well and was constantly in fellowship with Christ.

Yet he experienced a deep period of doubt. In his despair he wrote about an eclipse of faith; an eclipse of faith so daunting that he eventually left the ministry, although he later returned with new faith and vigor.

Read every word of his testimony:

To all of us who struggle with doubt, Lord, there are times when my experience is the experience of Thomas. There are days when I hear not the bells of Easter morn. I tread the road of Emmaus and meet not the Risen Christ. I stand on the mountain of Galilee and there comes no voice among the breezes. I sail on Galilee's lake and I see no vision. I frequent the upper room and get no hint of His presence. My faith cannot walk by sight in hours like these. Lord, what shall I do? Hast Thou a remedy for the loss of light? Yes, my Father, Thou hast a gate where faith can enter without seeing where it goes. Its name is love. Oh Lord, lead me by that gate when my eye is dim. When I cannot follow Him to Olivet, let me worship Him on Calvary. When I lose sight of His risen form, do not shut me out of the hearing and the bearing of His name. If I cannot soar with Him in heaven, let me at least go back to finish His work on earth. Let me mourn with the Marthas whose Lazaruses I cannot raise. Let me pray with the paralytics whose weakness I cannot cure. Let me sing to the sightless whose eyes I cannot open. Let me lend to the lepers the touch of a brother's hand. Let me find for the fallen a chance to renew their days. Then shall my Easter morn shine again through the clouds of night. Then shall I know the meaning of the words,

"Blessed are they who have not seen and yet have believed."[1]

Glimmers of faith in the midst of doubt!

PROOF POSITIVE!

Back to Thomas. He laid down the conditions that had to be met in order for him to believe. "Unless I see the nail marks in his hands and put my finger where the nails were, and put my hand into his side, I will not believe it" (John 20:25). The Greek construction of his statement leads us to believe that he was not expecting these conditions to be met. He honestly did not think that Jesus would meet the challenge. Whether Jesus appeared to His friends was an open question, but Thomas despaired that he would personally see Him.

A week later His disciples are gathered together again, and Thomas is present. As is their custom, the doors are locked to secure the room. Nevertheless, Jesus comes through the closed door without touching the lock. The molecular structure of His resurrected body is not deterred by matter. Jesus comes and stand among them and says, "Peace be with you!" And then He tells Thomas, "Put your finger here; see my hands. Reach out your hand and put it into my side. Stop doubting and believe" (v. 27).

Thomas exclaims, "My Lord and my God!"

"He's alive! I can't believe it, but my eyes see Him, and my hands are invited to touch Him!" Some Bible critics tell us that the stories of the New Testament were manufactured by the disciples, who were gullible men, anxious to take a mere man and make him into a god. They believed, we are told, on a wisp of evidence; they took a small story and made it into a miraculous one; they took a passing comment and turned it into a claim for deity.

Nonsense!

The disciples were hardheaded fishermen who would never have called a man God unless they had compelling reasons to do so. They were careful to not break the first commandment, "You shall have no other gods before me" (Exodus 20:3). To take a mere man and make him God would have been the highest form of blasphemy. The reason they believed Jesus was the Son of God was because the evidence was so overwhelming that they had little choice but to acknowledge His claims and believe His miracles. Only because the evidence could not be controverted did Thomas exclaim, "My Lord and my God!"

Why was Thomas convinced? First of all, because he was an *honest* doubter. If he'd been dishonest he would have said, "Even though Jesus appeared to me, it must have just been an apparition, or maybe I was hallucinating; in fact, maybe all of us are hallucinating. Come what may, I will not believe." Dishonest doubters are not convinced regardless of the evidence. As the old adage says, "Convince a man against his will and he will be of the same opinion still."

The great nineteenth-century British preacher Charles Haddon Spurgeon said that he would rather try to convince a tiger to eat straw than to try to convince a dishonest doubter to believe. A friend of mine has a myriad of objections to the Christian faith. If I answer one question, he has another; and if I answer that one, he has others. Of course I'm happy to spend time with honest doubters, but dishonest ones often cannot be helped. Perhaps because of bitterness or misconceptions, this man "has issues," as the current jargon goes. So he runs from the truth and its implications as fast as he can.

Do you remember the story about the man who believed he was dead? A psychiatrist who tried to disabuse him of this silliness taught him this simple truth, "Dead men don't bleed." So the doubter repeated the statement dozens of times a day, "Dead men don't bleed." Convinced that the man now understood, the psychiatrist took a pin and pricked his client's finger. Blood oozed out. But the doubter was not convinced and exclaimed, "Dead men bleed after all!"

Jesus said to Thomas, "Stop doubting and believe." And, because Thomas's doubt was honest, so too was his faith.

THE LOVE THAT WILL NOT LET US GO

Notice how personal Thomas's exclamation was: "*My* Lord and *my* God!" (italics added). Thomas was not speaking on behalf of the faith of the disciples, or the faith of his parents; this was a faith that was his.

Those who are reared in Christian homes often struggle with doubt: They ask themselves whether their faith is their own, or whether it is a borrowed faith, a faith that belongs to their church or their parents. We all have to make sure that our faith is our personal possession; we can learn from others and be inspired by them, but no one can believe for us. And, in the end, we discover that we are not merely cleaving to faith in Christ, but He is holding us, too.

George Matheson, whom we met a few pages back, wrote these words after his battle with doubt:

> *O Love that will not let me go,*
> *I rest my weary soul in Thee;*
> *I give Thee back the life I owe,*
> *That in Thine ocean depths its flow*
> *May richer, fuller be.*[2]

Doubts can overwhelm us, but Christ's love holds those who believe close to His heart.

You say, "Well, if I had a revelation like Thomas, I would believe, too!" Jesus knew that we might think that, so He commented, "Because you have seen me, you have believed; blessed are those who have not seen and yet have believed" (John 20:29). We've not had a revelation of Jesus like that of the disciples, but we are especially blessed if we believe even without such direct evidence.

Why do we believe? First, because of the witness of the apostles. They wrote down the biography of Jesus that can be verified by both archaeology and history. An honest look at the evidence shows that the Bible is a reliable document, rooted in the soil of history and reason.

Second, we believe because of those who have experienced the transforming power of Christ. Some of us can personally testify to changes that have happened in our lives that show the work of God from the inside out.

A prostitute who came to faith in Christ by attending a Sunday school class had her desires and attitude so completely changed that she was almost immediately freed from drugs and alcohol. Ten years later she ran a home for unwed mothers, providing the care and instruction they needed so that they could return to school. "Therefore, if anyone is in Christ, he is a new creation; the old has gone, the new has come!" (2 Corinthians 5:17).

WHEN NOT SEEING IS BELIEVING

Jesus invited Thomas to touch the scars on His hands and the healed wound on His side, because it was on the cross He offered Himself as a sacrifice for sinners to enable us to connect with God. The barrier of sin was removed for all who believe, and the invitation to be reconciled is made to all who wish to receive it. Whether our faith is great or small, we are invited to receive this gift by faith.

My name is not in the Bible, and neither is yours. Of course you might have a biblical name, but that's not what I mean. You and I are not mentioned as specific persons in the Bible. Perhaps this is the closest we will ever come in finding ourselves in the sacred writings, "Because you have seen me, you have believed; blessed are those who have not seen and yet have believed" (John 20:29). Blessed are you, Earl and Joanne, because though you have not seen, you have believed. Blessed are you, Harold and Charlene; though you have not seen, yet you have believed. Blessed are you, Phil and Pat. Blessed are you, dear reader; though you have not seen, you have believed.

I'm not concerned about whether you have doubts, as long as you are an honest doubter. Dishonest doubters throw up one smoke screen after another. They are determined not to believe; they relish skepticism and doubt as a sign of intelligence and savvy. An honest doubter is humble enough to pursue the truth wherever it leads. An honest doubter is willing to admit that he needs a Savior to set his sin aside so that fellowship with God becomes possible. An honest doubter can enter the doorway of doubt and emerge from the doorway of assurance.

Many years ago an invalid named Charlotte Elliott wrote a poem. Her brother, a pastor, said, "My sister has had a greater impact by writing this one single poem than all of my messages combined." This poem, called "Just as I Am,"[3] was put to music and is one of my favorite hymns. Perhaps you will recognize yourself in the third stanza.

> *Just as I am, though tossed about,*
> *With many a conflict, many a doubt;*
> *Fightings within and fears without,*
> *O Lamb of God, I come! I come!*

The fifth verse describes the wonderful, complete work of sacrifice accomplished by the Lamb.

> *Just as I am, Thou wilt receive,*
> *Wilt welcome, pardon, cleanse, relieve,*
> *Because Thy promise I believe,*
> *O Lamb of God, I come! I come!*

Thomas had his doubts but came to Christ. Let us join him—and we will be accepted too, embraced by the Love that never lets us go.

THE KEEPER OF THE KEYS

A Chicago newspaper carried a story about two young men who drowned in Lake Michigan. They were celebrating the return of one of them from the Persian Gulf War. They were drinking, lost control of their senses, and their boat overturned. Eventually their bodies were dragged from the lake.

Just imagine these young men, gasping for air, their lungs filling with water. They enter eternity sober, with their minds clearer and more aware than while on earth. They are conscious—all too conscious—of who they are, their families back in Chicago, and the opportunities they squandered. And with terrifying clarity they now know that they are without the power of significant choice.

No chance to better their situation by deadening their raw emotions with another drink. They have heightened desires without the ability to quench them.

Death robs us of the power of significant choice.

One minute after we die, we will no longer be able to choose our vocation; we will no longer be able to choose whether we will live in Dallas or Denver, or whether we will take a trip to Europe. Nor will we be able to choose where we will spend the rest of our eternity once it has officially begun!

Of course, in this life our choices are already quite limited. Yes, we can choose where we live, what we eat, and whom we marry (or not marry!). But we cannot choose to *not* live forever. There is virtually nothing we can do to prevent us from experiencing eternal existence. A thousand years from now, you will be more alive than you have ever been, and nothing you do today will change that fact.

Before people choose to commit suicide, they should meditate on the length of eternity. Their present misery seems to justify putting a period where there should only be a comma. But although some end this life by their own hands, they are helpless to end the life to come. They pass through a curtain only to discover that consciousness continues, either in a place of unimaginable bliss—or a place that we can only imagine as though it were a horror movie.

Hamlet, contemplating suicide, muttered, "In that sleep of death what dreams may come when we have shuffled off this mortal coil . . ."[1] Suicide is possible only in this life, not the next. On the other side we will have an indestructible body. We might have some choices within the framework of our new existence, but our fundamental status will be unchangeable. Some will have to adjust as best they can to eternal misery; others will joyfully adjust to eternal happiness and bliss. Only two places exist on the other side; only two kinds of people die; only two roads are before us.

Who determines which road we will take? Who determines where the drowned young men will spend eternity? Who has the authority to open the gate of heaven for some and to close it for others? How can we be assured of either heaven or hell? And how can a choice we make in this life determine our environment in the life to come?

GLORY AND GRANDEUR

Everyone has an opinion about Jesus. Most think of Him as a great teacher who welcomed little children to sit on His lap. He is remembered as the One who touched a sorrowing leper and the One who used the lunch of a little boy to feed a crowd of thousands. We think we have nothing to fear from this Jesus, who in the words of a familiar hymn is described as "meek and mild."

But after His resurrection, Jesus is seen in a different—and dazzling—light. In a vision, the apostle John saw Him in a robe that reached down to His feet. Then followed this: "His head and hair were white like wool, as white as snow, and his eyes were like blazing fire. His feet were like bronze glowing in a furnace, and his voice was like the sound of rushing waters. In his right hand he held seven stars, and out of his mouth came a sharp double-edged sword. His face was like the sun shining in all its brilliance" (Revelation 1:14–16).

"The sun shining in all its brilliance"! Consider: A mere one pound of heat energy is enough to take twenty million tons of rocks and increase their temperature to 2,500 degrees! If but one pound of heat will turn such rocks into lava, think of the heat of the sun that radiates four million tons of energy per second! We can't get our minds around such power, but this should help us grasp the awesome grandeur of the risen Christ.

No wonder John fell at His feet as though dead. But Jesus then placed His right hand on him and said, "Do not be afraid. I am the First and the Last. I am the Living One; I was dead, and behold I am alive for ever and ever! And I hold the keys of death and Hades" (vv. 17–18).

Here Jesus parts company with other would-be saviors. Here Jesus is revealed as more than simply a wise teacher or kind shepherd. He alone has the authority to open the door of paradise for some— and close it for others.

THE BEGINNING AND THE END

Just before his vision, John recorded Jesus as saying, "I am the Alpha and the Omega, . . . who is, and who was, and who is to come, the Almighty" (1:8). Alpha is the first letter of the Greek alphabet (yes, you noticed the word in *alpha*bet), and omega is the last letter. We would say that Jesus is the A to Z, and, of course, He is everything in between. The *Encyclopedia Britannica* comes in twenty-six volumes, yet all of these articles in history, science, geography, and the like are all written with an alphabet of twenty-six letters. Jesus is the A and the Z, and in Him "are hidden all the treasures of wisdom and knowledge" (Colossians 2:3).

Jesus claims existence in all three time frames. He is the God of the past: "I am the Alpha . . . who was." He is the beginning of all things: He existed before anything else. He was in the beginning, because He did not have a beginning. If someone asks you who created God, the answer is that He had no creator; He always was.

Now, I know we can't comprehend how a Being

can exist from all eternity, but your own existence is proof that it is so. Think this through: If there were no being that eternally existed in the past, nothing would exist in the present. If in the beginning there were nothing, there would not be something today, for out of nothing, nothing comes! Even on rational grounds, we have to conclude that Christ is eternal.

So much for His past existence. As for the present, "I am the Living One; I was dead" (Revelation 1:18). Yes, He actually was dead, so dead that His body was laid in a cold tomb. We've seen that Mary Magdalene and several other women came to anoint His body and see if they could do a better job of the burial. When they arrived, they found the stone rolled away, but Jesus was nowhere to be found.

What happened to Jesus while His body was in the tomb? The Apostles' Creed says that Jesus "descended into Hades." If so, He was there for only a brief moment, for that very day He was on hand to welcome the dying thief into paradise. But because He died, He knows what lies on the other side of the grave.

Today, research is conducted to try to probe death with the intention of investigating life beyond the grave. We've all read stories of "near-death experiences" where people return to tell us about visions of light and beauty. But such information is suspect, because to be *near* death is not the same as *being* dead; to be at the door is not the same as going through the door and then having it lock behind us.

As for His future, Jesus said, "I am alive forever and ever!" Jesus did not just appear to His disciples; He was raised not just for them, but also for us. In fact, someday we too shall see the resurrected Jesus, appearing with power and great glory.

THE ONE WITH THE KEYS

The Key to Hades

Christ's resurrection qualifies Him to be the only One who holds the keys of "death and Hades."

Keys are a symbol of authority. I have a key for our church building; in fact, my key will not only get me into the building but also into the office area and into my study. I have access to all parts of the building; there is no area where I am excluded.

To the ancient church in Philadelphia, Jesus said, "These are the words of him who is holy and true, who holds the key of David. What he opens no one can shut, and what he shuts no one can open" (Revelation 3:7). Be assured that no door is closed to Jesus. He can enter any country, any home . . . or any heart. What He opens stays open; what He closes stays closed.

Visualize a huge castle with only one entrance

through which every human being must pass at death. As we pass through the gate, Jesus stands just on the other side to open one of two doors: the door that leads to eternal life or the door to eternal death. The doors open and close at His command, and there is no opportunity for negotiations. At death our destiny is unalterably fixed.

"I hold the keys of death and Hades" (Revelation 1:18). The Old Testament taught that Sheol was the abode of spirits; it was a place of dreariness and darkness, a place of misery, which could not be alleviated by sacrifices and prayers. Interestingly, there is also evidence that it also had a righteous side; thus, although the wicked and the righteous were separated, they existed next to one another.

This "two-compartment theory," as it is called, seems clear from the New Testament, where the word *Hades* is used to translate the Hebrew word *Sheol*. Jesus told a story about the rich man and Lazarus in Luke 16:22–26. "The time came when the beggar died and the angels carried him to Abraham's side. The rich man also died and was buried. In hell, where he was in torment, he looked up and saw Abraham far away, with Lazarus by his side." Then we are told the rich man "called to him, 'Father Abraham, have pity on me and send Lazarus to dip the tip of his finger in water and cool my tongue, because I am in agony in this fire.'"

The conversation continued, with Abraham

himself responding to the man's pitiful plea, "'Son, remember that in your lifetime you received your good things, while Lazarus received bad things, but now he is comforted here and you are in agony. And besides all this, between us and you a great chasm has been fixed, so that those who want to go from here to you cannot, nor can anyone cross over from there to us.'"

Two thousand years have passed, and this miserable man has not yet received the drop of water for which he longed.

So it appears that back then hades contained both paradise and the dark, dreary judgment of suffering and misery. After the resurrection of Jesus, paradise seems to have been moved to heaven, and hades is exclusively the haunting abode of those who have not received God's forgiveness.

So who determined that the rich man would go to hades and Lazarus to the place that would be called paradise? Jesus, of course. In fact, Jesus still opens the door of hades today for those who reject His forgiveness. That door shall be swung wide open after the final judgment. Just read this terrifying account:

Then I saw a great white throne and him who was seated on it. Earth and sky fled from his presence, and there was no place for them. And I saw the dead, great and small, standing before the throne, and books were

THE VANISHING POWER OF DEATH

*opened. Another book was opened, which is the book of
life. The dead were judged according to what they had
done as recorded in the books. The sea gave up the dead
that were in it, and death and Hades gave up the dead
that were in them, and each person was judged according to what he had done. Then death and Hades were
thrown into the lake of fire. The lake of fire is the second
death. If anyone's name was not found written in the
book of life, he was thrown into the lake of fire.* (Revelation 20:11–15)

"Death and Hades . . . thrown into the lake of
fire"! The door to hades, and to hell, for that matter, cannot be opened apart from the authority of
Jesus. Whether opened for one person or for the
hordes that will press through it in the final judgment, Jesus holds the key to the life beyond.

The Key to Paradise

That Jesus has the key to paradise is proven by
His words to the thief on the cross, "Today you will
be with me in paradise" (Luke 23:43). This man—
who was Jesus' last companion on earth—was His
first companion in heaven. Imagine the authority
that Jesus has: To this bad-to-the-bone thief, Jesus
made the same promise as that given to His disciples. This dying man is as surely in heaven as the
saints who have walked with God all of their lives.

Sometimes Jesus opens the door for the young to enter paradise. Jim Elliot, who was martyred back in 1956, said, "I must not think it strange if God takes in youth those whom I would have kept on earth until they were older. God is peopling heaven; why should he limit himself to old folks? " Young and old leave this earth and enter heaven at the bidding of the One who holds the keys of death and hades.

In the book *One Minute After You Die*, I tell a story of the Reverend A. D. Sandborn, who called on a young Christian woman who was seriously ill. She was bolstered up in bed, almost in a sitting position. She looked off into the distance where she spotted a gate.

"Now just as soon as they open the gate, I will go in," she whispered.

Then she sank upon her pillow in disappointment. "They have let Mamie go in ahead of me, but soon I will go in."

Moments later, she spoke again, "They let Grandpa in ahead of me, but next time I will go in for sure." No one spoke to her and she said nothing more to anyone, and seemed to see nothing except the sights of the beautiful city. Reverend Sandborn then left the house because of the press of other duties.

Later in the day the pastor learned that the

young woman had died. He was so impressed with what she had said that he asked the family about the identity of Mamie and Grandpa. Mamie was a little girl who had lived near them at one time but later moved to New York State. As for Grandpa, he was a friend of the family and had moved somewhere in the Southwest.

Reverend Sandborn then wrote to the addresses given to him. Much to his astonishment, he discovered that both Mamie and Grandpa had died the morning of September 16, the very hour that the young woman herself had passed into glory! [2]

"Death is not the end of the road, but a bend in the road." [3] Whether hades or paradise, Jesus has the keys for both.

Your Turn to Meet Jesus

Every human being must meet this "Keeper of the Keys." No atheist can die unnoticed by Jesus. Hindus, Muslims, Christians—no matter religion or creed, none can escape this divine appointment. Jesus waits for everyone, either as Savior or Judge.

Sadly, many people expecting to enter paradise will find its door shut in their faces. "Many will say to me on that day, 'Lord, Lord, did we not prophesy in your name, and in your name drive out demons and perform many miracles?' Then I will tell them plainly, 'I never knew you. Away from me, you evil-doers!'" (Matthew 7:22–23). For these people, the door to paradise will be closed and the door to hades will be opened—a door that according to Dante has inscribed above it the warning "Abandon All Hope Ye Who Enter Here."

In British Columbia, a couple hundred miles north of Vancouver, the Frazier River hits an outcropping of rock. From there it divides into two smaller rivers, one of which flows to the Atlantic, the other to the Pacific. Little wonder that place is known as "the Great Divide." Just so, we rush along to our inevitable appointment with Jesus, and some shall be escorted to the right and some to the left. "Then they will go away to eternal punishment, but the righteous to eternal life" (Matthew 25:46). Once separated, never the twain shall meet.

Mind you, those who are escorted to hades will not evade worshiping Jesus. We read that (whether willingly or unwillingly), "at the name of Jesus every knee should bow, in heaven and on earth and under the earth, and every tongue confess that Jesus Christ is Lord, to the glory of God the Father" (Philippians 2:10–11). Their worship will not change their destiny, but nonetheless it will bring honor to the only One who is worthy of adoration and praise. God the Father adores His Son so much that He would not allow so much as a single person to depart His presence without acknowledging Jesus as Lord and King.

A father was staying at a hotel with his baby daughter, who took sick and died. He bought a small casket for her and then called a minister for a funeral. Together they drove to the cemetery, where the keeper of the cemetery joined them. For one last time, the father looked upon the face of his precious child; then she was lowered into her grave. He then gave the key of the casket to the keeper of the cemetery.

On the way back to the hotel, the father was weeping, while the minister comforted him. "You think that the keeper of the cemetery has the key to your little girl's casket, but I want you to know that that is not true." Then he read this text: "I am the First and the Last. I am the Living One; I was dead, and behold I am alive for ever and ever! And I hold the keys of death and Hades" (Revelation 1:17–18).

No one enters paradise without a welcome from Jesus. No one is admitted unless his or her faith is in Him as the only qualified Savior. He holds the keys, and no one shall wrest them from His nail-pierced hand. He was dead and is alive forevermore, amen!

CHAPTER SIX

DYING IN THE CARE OF JESUS

American Baby Boomers still are whining because scientists have not yet developed a cure for death," columnist John Kass wrote in the *Chicago Tribune*. We can be quite sure that the whining will continue, for a cure for death is beyond the realm of the scientific enterprise. "Sin entered the world through one man, and death through sin, and in this way death came to all men, because all sinned" (Romans 5:12).

If Jesus is Lord, if He is worthy of our trust, He must triumph here, or we shall be forever disappointed. To turn water into wine, to feed a crowd with a lunch, or to open the eyes of the blind makes little difference in the face of that which matters most.

One Thanksgiving Day my wife and I had just sat down at a table with some friends when the phone rang. The wife of a friend had collapsed at her dinner table and died. The next week, another friend died just a mile from his home while jogging. Whenever death comes, laughter is turned into mourning; the anticipation of joy turns into deep shock and sorrow.

We all want to be assured that Jesus will walk with us as we pass through the parted curtain. We want to know that He is committed to us on this side of the grave and beyond. We need the confidence that we can entrust both soul and body to His loving care. For our ultimate experience, we need an ultimate Savior.

In this chapter we turn from the tomb of Jesus to see Him weep at the tomb of a friend. Even before His own resurrection, He proved that He has the power over death. Strictly speaking, the resurrection of Lazarus was actually resuscitation, because he was not raised with a glorified body but simply restored to an earthly existence. In point of fact, he had to die all over again!

We turn to this story because we want to have a better understanding of how Jesus views death; we want to understand how He interpreted the death of a friend so that we can better understand Jesus' perspective of our own death—whenever that will occur. We want to be assured that we will die in His care.

"Now a man named Lazarus was sick. He was from Bethany, the village of Mary and her sister Martha" (John 11:1). This was the Mary who sat at Jesus' feet, listening to His words. This was the Martha who was "worried and upset about many things" (Luke 10:41). John continues, "This Mary, whose brother Lazarus now lay sick, was the same one who poured perfume on the Lord and wiped his feet with her hair" (John 11:2).

DEATH FROM JESUS' PERSPECTIVE

This was a family who loved Jesus—and who was loved by Him. Yet death comes into every home, including those in which Jesus is loved. In this story we are given a glimpse into the home of grieving sisters but also a glimpse into the heart of Jesus. Here love and sorrow meet.

We Die with the Assurance of God's Love

The sisters sent word to Jesus, saying simply, "Lord, the one you love is sick." Surprisingly, He replies to the messengers, "This sickness will not end in death. No, it is for God's glory so that God's Son may be glorified through it." Then John adds this bit of commentary: "Jesus loved Martha and her sister and Lazarus" (vv. 3–5).

Jesus loved Lazarus—but Lazarus still got sick and died. God's love toward us does not mean we will be spared the passing through the iron gate that opens only in one direction. We might feel forsaken by God, but He is there; His love abides with us into eternity. Our suffering is not inconsistent with the love of God.

Jesus also loved the two sisters. They were concerned about their future: How would the family get along, now that the sole provider for the family was gone? As word spread throughout the little village of Bethany, the neighbors shared their concerns.

Incredibly, Jesus, who loved this family, did not hurry to Bethany. "Yet when he heard that Lazarus was sick, he stayed where he was two more days" (v. 6). No hurry to prevent the death of his friend; no hurry to give comfort to the grieving sisters.

When Jesus finally arrived in Bethany, Lazarus had already been dead for four days. Let's think through the sequence of events. Just possibly, Lazarus died when the messenger arrived with the news for Jesus. Then Jesus stayed in the Transjordan region for two days before He began the two-day trek to Bethany. This would account for the four days.

While the messenger was gone, the sisters sat

waiting for a miracle. But the clammy sweat of death gathered on their brother's brow. His body filled with anguish and pain, and at last he passed into the life beyond. The sisters wept over his lifeless body, and, according to custom, his corpse was wrapped in a shroud and buried within twenty-four hours.

When the messenger returned, Lazarus had already been dead for two days. I can imagine him conveying the words of Jesus, "This sickness will not end in death" to the grieving sisters. They must have pondered these words, unsure what they could possibly mean. At this point, the sickness did indeed "end in death," for their brother was in the grave. Exactly what Jesus meant would become clear later. They took comfort in the fact that this sickness was "for the glory of God." But they could not reconcile the promise with their brother's sudden demise.

We'd like to have an answer to this question: Can we be sure God loves us even when we face death? In the face of unbearable suffering, does God withdraw His hand? Is His refusal to come to our aid proof that we can't count on His love? Paul answers with a definitive *no*.

Who shall separate us from the love of Christ? Shall trouble or hardship or persecution or famine or nakedness or danger or sword? . . . No, in all these things we

*are more than conquerors through him who loved us.
For I am convinced that neither death nor life, neither
angels nor demons, neither the present nor the future,
nor any powers, neither height nor depth, nor anything
else in all creation, will be able to separate us from the
love of God that is in Christ Jesus our Lord.* (Romans
8:35, 37–39)

Like Lazarus, we also die with the assurance of
Jesus' love. Our death, even if it should be sooner
than expected, does not cancel out Jesus' care for
us. Indeed, death is the chariot He sends to take us
home to be with Him. His love draws us from earth
to heaven.

We Die Within the Circle of God's Providence

Why did Jesus not hurry to Bethany? Was His decision to wait a heartless response to the urgent cry
of His beloved friends? Verbally, He is encouraging
—"This sickness will not end in death"—but His
actions are confusing. He does not hurry but lingers,
long enough for Lazarus to die and be buried.

After two days, Jesus tells the disciples that they
must return to Judea, the territory where Bethany was
located. The disciples warn Him that the Jews tried
to stone him on their last visit in Judea. Jesus, confi-
dent that He will be protected by the will of God,
reminds them that to walk in obedience is to walk in

the daylight; to walk at night; that is, out of God's will, is indeed dangerous. To walk without confidence in the will of God would lead to stumbling.

"Our friend Lazarus has fallen asleep; but I am going there to wake him up" (John 11:11). Then Jesus explains that Lazarus was not just sleeping but that he had died. "So then he told them plainly, 'Lazarus is dead, and for your sake I am glad I was not there, so that you may believe. But let us go to him'" (v. 14).

"I am glad I was not there"!

The words seem out of place. Martha and Mary are weeping, but Jesus is *glad;* the disciples are filled with fear, but Jesus is *glad!* Of course, He is not glad because of sorrow but glad because of what sorrow does within the human heart.

Why does Jesus not spare Martha her bitter tears? Why is He not moved to action by the sorrow that threatens to break Mary's tender heart? Why does He not speak the word at a distance and let the flush of health return to Lazarus' cheeks?

Spurgeon has given the best answer to these questions. "Christ is not glad because of sorrow, but on account of the result of it. He [knows] this temporary trial [will] help His disciples to a greater faith, and He so prizes their growth in faith that He is even glad of the sorrow which occasions it. . . . He sets so high a value upon His people's faith, that He will not screen them from those trials by which faith is strengthened."[1]

The love of God does not necessarily result in health, wealth, and happy relationships. Jesus is touched by the feelings of our infirmities, but He does not shield us from those trials that will develop the qualities He so values. The delays of Deity are not because of insensitivity to our *present* needs, but because of greater sensitivity to our *ultimate* needs. There are benefits in those tears.

When He arrives in Bethany, the word spreads, and Martha runs to greet Him.

"Lord," she says, "if you had been here, my brother would not have died. But I know that even now God will give you whatever you ask."

"Your brother will rise again," Jesus tells her (vv. 21–23).

"I know he will rise again in the resurrection at the last day."

"I am the resurrection and the life. He who believes in me will live, even though he dies; and whoever lives and believes in me will never die. Do you believe this?"

"Yes, Lord. . . . I believe that you are the Christ, the Son of God, who was to come into the world" (vv. 24–27).

Martha runs back to the house to tell her sister that Jesus has come to town. Mary runs to meet him, saying the same words, "Lord, *if* you had been here, my brother would not have died" (v. 32, italics added).

"If only . . ." At almost every funeral I've attended, I have heard, "If only . . ."

"*If only* I had convinced him to go to the doctor sooner."

"*If only* he had not been driving that evening."

"*If only* they had not operated on him."

"*If only* . . ."

What shall we do with our "if onlys"?

Jesus would tell us that we must believe that these happenstances are a part of God's sovereign purposes and plan. If we could represent all of our "if onlys" as dots on a sheet of paper, we must then draw a circle large enough to encompass all of them. And that circle represents the providence of God.

We do not know the cause of Lazarus' illness. Perhaps it was a disease, a weak heart, or a bad case of the flu. Whatever, these infirmities were the immediate cause of his death; but the ultimate cause is God. He is the One who can take life or prolong it; He is the One who determines the length of our days. That which is out of our control is firmly within His grasp. No sickness, accident, or bolt of lightning can take us from this life if God still has work for us to do.

THE CARING JESUS

When Jesus saw the sisters weeping and the Jews who had come along with them weeping, He was "deeply moved in spirit and troubled" (v. 33). They brought Him to the grave.

"Jesus wept" (v. 35).

In those two words, we see most poignantly the humanity of the Son of God. This is proof, if more proof were needed, that the portrait of Jesus given in the Gospels was not manufactured by wild-eyed disciples who were burning with messianic fever. If anyone had used his or her imagination to write a biography of God in the flesh, all biographers would have thought Him too far removed from our experiences to weep.

If you and I had been making up the story of Jesus, we would have created a dry-eyed Messiah who refused to weep, because, after all, He understood the eternal purposes of God. Our Jesus would have been above the emotional roller coaster of mere mortals. Tears belong to us but not to Him.

Yes, Jesus was the Christ, the Son of the living God. He was more than a man, to be sure, but a man nevertheless. If you had taken a sample of His tears, they would have had the same chemical composition as your own. He is touched with the feeling of our infirmities, and He weeps.

"Jesus wept."

Here we have Jesus entering into the pain of mortals. "Jesus, once more deeply moved, came to the tomb. It was a cave with a stone laid across the entrance" (v. 38).

THE OMNIPOTENT CHRIST

"Take away the stone," He commanded.

"But, Lord," said Martha, the sister of the dead man, "by this time there is a bad odor, for he has been there four days" (v. 39). Would it have been easier to resurrect Lazarus if he had been dead for just one day, or even one hour? Would being in the grave ten years or ten centuries make it more difficult? No, dead is dead, and only God can bring the dead back to life.

"Did I not tell you that if you believed, you would see the glory of God?" (v. 40). For the world, seeing is believing; for those who trust Jesus, believing is seeing.

This verse has sometimes been misused to teach that we can see whatever miracle we want if only we believe and desire to see the glory of God. But again we have to remember that this was a specific promise regarding a specific situation. Jesus is referring to the words He gave to the messenger that "this sickness will not end in death. No, it is for God's glory so that God's Son may be glorified through it" (v. 4). Jesus did not mean that the disease would not be fatal but that it would end in resurrection. The sisters had reason to believe and see the glory of God.

So they took the stone away. The One who stood at the tomb could have spoken a word, and the stone would have been removed to wherever omnipotence wished to send it. But the Master willed that His friends be a part of the miracle. They could not restore Lazarus to his sisters, but they could take the stone away. We've learned that there are some things we can do and some things only God can do. Blessed are those who can tell the difference.

Then Jesus prayed, saying words that were as much directed toward those who were standing next to Him as to the heavenly Father Himself. The prayer implies that He and His Father had agreed on this plan in the ages long ago. Before He stepped out of eternity into time at Bethlehem, this moment was already a part of the divine plan. Indeed, it was scarcely necessary to pray the words, since the outcome was certain. Let's listen as the Son speaks to His Father.

"Father, I thank you that you have heard me. I knew that you always hear me, but I said this for the benefit of the people standing here, that they may believe that you sent me" (vv. 41–42). The will of the Father and the prayer of the Son were united in one heart and purpose.

Then He called in a loud voice, "Lazarus, come out!" (v. 43).

Augustine in the fourth century said that it was good that Jesus called Lazarus by name, or else all corpses in the cemetery would have arisen! Jesus was saying, "Lazarus, this way out!" He was directing Lazarus out of the cavern. He wanted to make sure that they knew that this was the same man they had buried four days ago.

"The dead man came out, his hands and feet wrapped with strips of linen, and a cloth around his face. Jesus said to them, 'Take off the grave clothes and let him go'" (v. 44).

His sisters and his startled friends embraced Lazarus. If he remembered what death was like, it mattered not at this moment. His fondest memories were drowned in a chorus of celebrations. The God by whose providence he died is the God by whose providence he lived.

OUR DEATH SERVES GOD'S PURPOSE

Why had Jesus stayed away when told that Lazarus was ill? We've learned that He said that this sickness would not end in death but that "God's Son may be glorified." The glory of God takes precedence over our health; it is more important that the glory of God be served than that we are free of sorrow. God's glory is all that matters.

How was the Son of God glorified in the death of Lazarus?

First, Jesus proved He has the power to reverse the process of death. "Where, O death, is your victory? Where, O death, is your sting?" (1 Corinthians 15:55).

A healed Lazarus would have been a great miracle; a resurrected Lazarus was an even greater one. Death has been conquered.

Second, Jesus desired to build faith in the lives of His followers. He was glad for what the sorrow accomplished. To quote Spurgeon once more, "He is glad for your sakes that your husband is taken away, that your child is buried; glad that your business does not prosper; He is glad that you have those pains and aches, and that you have so weak a body, to the intent that you may believe."[2]

In some tribes in Africa, Christians pray that they will have a "good death." By that they do not mean that they will die without pain and suffering, but that they will have peace in their sickness and thereby urge their relatives and friends to be faithful in their service for the Lord. God is glorified when we are satisfied with His plan, even His plan for our death.

Third, it substantiated Jesus' claim "I am the resurrection and the life. He who believes in me will live, even though he dies; and whoever lives and believes in me will never die" (John 11:25–26). When we die, our physical body accelerates the process of decomposition. But the promise is that we will live even though we die. And if we are alive spiritually, we never really die at all. This is not a denial of death (as Christian Science would maintain); it is recognition that when the physical body dies, the life Jesus gives us guarantees a glorious future existence.

Jesus does not say, "I *give* resurrection life," but rather, "I *am* the resurrection and the life." Once we grasp who He is, it is not difficult to believe what He can do. He who has triumphed over physical death has the power to triumph over spiritual death too. Jesus said Lazarus was sleeping, not because the soul sleeps but because the body "sleeps" until the day of resurrection. And when we are raised, it will not be with a resuscitated body like Lazarus' that had to die again, but with a glorious body like Jesus' that will never perish. "We shall be like him, for we shall see him as he is" (1 John 3:2).

The resurrection of Lazarus gives us one more reason to believe that we have a qualified Savior. We do not have a Savior who can just "help" us. We need a Savior who can resurrect us. We do not need a Savior just for the difficult experiences of life but a Savior who is there for us when life ends. For believers, death is transitional, not terminal. When God gives us "dying grace," we are a witness to His forgiveness and power. Death is a time of transition, not annihilation.

I wish I could have interviewed Lazarus the day after his resurrection. I'm sure he would have been free of fear. Tell him that he might be killed later, and he would laugh, "Been there, done that!" No sickness, no disease, no accident could have made him afraid. He had been to paradise and back and longed to return. And when he died again, his body was put into the tomb, awaiting its final glorification.

The experience of Lazarus illustrates the conversion of a sinner. We are dead "in trespasses and sins," and Jesus makes us alive. We are then set free of our grave clothes; that is, we are freed from the debilitating effects of sin, and we are invited to sit with Jesus at supper (see John 12:1–3).

William Barclay quotes the dying words of Edward the Confessor, king of England and builder of the first Westminster Abbey in A.D. 1000: "Weep not, I shall not die; and as I leave the land of the dying, I trust to see the blessings of the Lord in the land of the living. We call this world the land of the living; but it would be in fact more correct to call it the land of the dying. Through Jesus Christ we know that we are journeying, not to the sunset, but to the sunrise."[3]

Do you believe this?

Much of this chapter first appeared as chapter 7 of the book Seven Convincing Miracles, *by Erwin Lutzer (Moody, 1999).*

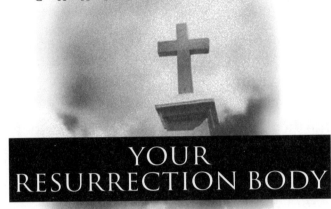

CHAPTER SEVEN

YOUR RESURRECTION BODY

Recently I conducted a funeral for Aimie, a thirteen-year-old girl who had struggled with muscular dystrophy. Eventually the muscles around her heart were no longer able to function, and she quietly slipped into the arms of Jesus.

Her body was tenderly laid in a coffin that was lowered into the ground. Her spirit was taken to heaven, and there in His presence she could walk, talk, and sing. We can be quite sure that, having seen Jesus, Aimie would not want to return to earth, even if she could.

And yet, whatever kind of body she has today, it is not her final habitation. Aimie's glorified body will be given to her when Christ returns, and at that time her human spirit will be united with it. "For the Lord himself will come down from heaven, with a loud command, with the voice of the archangel and with the trumpet call of God, and the dead in Christ will rise first. After that, we who are still alive and are left will be caught up together with them in the clouds to meet the Lord in the air. And so we will be with the Lord forever" (1 Thessalonians 4:16–17).

NEW BODIES

After His resurrection, Jesus passed through locked doors, traveled instantly from one location to another, and ascended into heaven in His resurrected body. If indeed we shall be like Him, we must ask: What kind of a body will we have at the resurrection?

Let me make a few points of clarification.

First, I do not believe that our new bodies will be created *ex nihilo*, that is, out of nothing. Obviously God could do it that way, but consider: Why was the tomb of Jesus empty? God used Christ's earthly body and re-created it for its heavenly existence. Jesus was not only recognized after His resurrection, but He could be identified by the nail prints in His hands and a spear wound in His side.

If we had been eyewitnesses to the Resurrection, what would we have seen? Would we have witnessed His eyes open and adjust to the darkness, then seen Him gradually pull Himself out of the grave clothes, and then stand groping for the sides of the tomb? No, we would have seen the body of Jesus disappear and simultaneously reappear, lifting itself through the walls of the tomb. John Stott says that the body was "vaporized, being transmuted into something new and different and wonderful." The linen clothes would have collapsed, lying quite undisturbed where the body of Jesus had lain.

"But"—I can hear the argument—"our bodies are constantly in flux; cells die and re-create themselves with relentless consistency. Jesus was in the tomb only three days, but our bodies decay and return to the dust. Bodies buried for centuries, or bodies that have been burned, have returned back to nature with no discernible identity even on scientific grounds."

I reply that yes, it is so, but God is able to retrieve the particles and re-create them as He deems fit.

Interestingly, when the great masses of humanity are raised for their final judgment, we read, "The sea gave up the dead that were in it" (Revelation 20:13). Obviously, bodies drowned centuries ago have long since decomposed or have been eaten by sharks and other sea creatures. Yet, in some way God "raised" these bodies from their resting place so that they could be re-created in their final form.

Second, we must keep in mind that our new body will have similar functions to that of our present body. After His resurrection, Jesus walked, talked, and even ate fish on the shores of Galilee. Yet, despite these similarities, Paul the apostle chooses to emphasize the differences.

OUR BODIES TODAY, OUR BODIES TOMORROW

In 1 Corinthians 15 Paul makes four contrasts between our present physical bodies and the ones we shall enjoy in the resurrection. He likens our old body to a seed that was sown in the ground that will come up and be re-created as our permanent dwelling place. As we think about our own physical limitations, we can hardly imagine the body we shall someday have.

The Perishable Versus the Imperishable

"So will it be with the resurrection of the dead. The body that is sown is perishable, it is raised imperishable" (1 Corinthians 15:42). Today our bodies are subject to decay and disintegration; our particles are moving toward randomness and decomposition. We begin to die the moment we are born.

When God warned Adam not to eat of the forbidden tree, "for when you eat of it you will surely die" (Genesis 2:17), Adam disobeyed and died. He died spiritually in that he was cut off from God, but he also died physically, for in that moment the journey to the grave had begun. Now we live in perishable bodies, ever moving toward the final slowdown.

However, we shall be raised imperishable; that is, our future bodies will be indestructible. There will be no aging in heaven. You will look as young ten thousand years from now as you will a thousand years from now. We will never outgrow our clothes and our habitat. If we fear boredom because of the constancy of heaven, we need only remind ourselves that God will have plenty for us to do.

We should note in passing that the same quality of indestructibility will be true of the bodies of those who end in the lake of fire. Their bodies will not be destroyed by the flames; suicide will be impossible. We catch a glimpse of this in the book of Revelation when men in their present bodies are unable to end their lives according to their own timetable. "During those days men will seek death, but will not find it; they will long to die, but death will elude them" (Revelation 9:6). Eventually, they will die, of course, but when resurrected they will discover continued and increased frustration: There will be no escape from their terrifying existence.

Contrast the plight of the unconverted with the anticipation of those who have embraced Christ as

Savior. When Reverend W. B. Hinson, longtime pastor in Portland, Oregon, discovered he had a terminal disease, he walked outside of the city where he could see Mount Hood. Then he looked at a river, and in the evening he gazed at the stars. Finally he said, "I may not see you many more times, but Mountain, I shall be alive when you are gone; and River, I shall be alive when you cease running toward the sea; and Stars, I shall be alive when you have fallen from your sockets in the great down pulling of the material universe!"[1]

An unknown poet wrote,

> *The stars shall live for a million years,*
> *A million years and a day,*
> *But God and I will live and love*
> *When the stars have passed away.*

The perishable will become imperishable.

Dishonor Versus Glory

This earthly body is "sown in dishonor, it is raised in glory" (1 Corinthians 15:43). At death, we put a covering over the body to shield our eyes from the indignity of the corpse. We are grateful for undertakers who do their best to make the corpse presentable for the funeral. But nothing can remove the disgrace of death. I believe it was C. S. Lewis who said that the most beautiful corpse cannot compare with the most decrepit, but living, body.

I was asked to speak at a funeral of a family that evidently knew nothing of God's saving grace. In order to comfort the grieving mother, a friend stared into the coffin and said, "Just look at Mabel; she is wearing a party dress. She looks so good, just as if she was going to a party!" But even the beautiful party dress could not hide the putrefaction of death. The curse of God stamps the dead body with mournful disgrace.

In contrast, our resurrected body will be one of shining splendor and glory. Think of Moses and Elijah on the Mount of Transfiguration. Every blemish is removed, every limitation is overcome, and every wish for health and strength is granted. Here is strength, beauty, and dignity. This body is built to last.

Sometimes I'm asked whether the crippled will be so in heaven. Of course not; every imperfection will be replaced with grace and glory. And what about babies? Perhaps God will create their bodies to look like they would have been if they had grown to normal size. Of this we can be sure: Our bodies will have the blessedness of Jesus Himself.

Our culture tells us that if we do not meet artificial standards of beauty, we will simply not rate in society. Getting a mate or being accepted by our peers is dependent on appearance. We spend billions of dollars on various diets and cosmetic surgery in the vain hope we will look more attractive, younger, more desirable. But at the resurrection we will have no thought of such competition—because all of us will be like Christ! We all will be equally beautiful, all equally glorious. At last our quest for acceptance will have come to an end.

"To him who overcomes, I will give the right to sit with me on my throne, just as I overcame and sat down with my Father on his throne. He who has an ear, let him hear what the Spirit says to the churches" (Revelation 3:21–22).

Weakness Versus Strength

Paul continued regarding the believer's body, "It is sown in weakness, it is raised in power" (1 Corinthians 15:43). Come with me to the hospital, and let's walk from room to room. Here's a man forty years old recovering from open-heart surgery. He is trying to manage his depression and wondering whether his recovery will be successful. He is also worried because he has been unemployed for several months, so he does not know how his wife and children will survive the economic downturn. Known for his strength, he is now reduced to needing the help of nurses to get out of bed.

In the next room is a young thirty-something

mother who has just been told that she has terminal cancer. The news has tormented her mind and
weakened her body. She can only think of her two
children and wonders how they will be cared for.
Her ex-husband is devastated, giving every sign that
he is unable to cope emotionally with the news. He
thinks about what this will mean for him and the
children who will fall to his care. He does not think
he has the strength to go on.

By the time we have walked through a single
hallway, even those of us who are healthy feel tired.
We leave the hospital, determined that we will do
our best to stave off death for another day, a week,
or a year. Like it or not, weakness shall eventually
overtake us too.

But we shall be raised with power! Jesus was
able to move from Galilee to Jerusalem—and pass
through closed doors, no less—without effort! Evidently with our new bodies, the *thought* will be the
action. If you want to move from one place to
another in the New Jerusalem, you only have to
think where you would like to be—and you will be
there. In heaven there will be no sun and no moon,
because the glory of God shall enlighten it. What
this means is that there will be no need for sleep,
for we shall never be weary, never out of breath,
and never in need of a vacation. At last we shall
have our twenty-four-hour day without feeling
overworked.

Let the weariness we feel today be a reminder that we shall never feel such again for all of eternity. The land of perpetual strength lies in our future.

Natural Versus Spiritual

There is a final contrast: "It is sown a natural body, it is raised a spiritual body" (1 Corinthians 15:44). By *natural,* Paul means sensual; he means our desires that constantly get in the way of our fulfillment will no longer trouble us. Even such basic drives as hunger and thirst will no longer interrupt our schedules and opportunities for service. "Never again will they hunger; never again will they thirst. The sun will not beat upon them, nor any scorching heat. For the Lamb at the center of the throne will be their shepherd; he will lead them to springs of living water. And God will wipe away every tear from their eyes" (Revelation 7:16–17).

In contrast, those who suffer in what the Bible calls "the lake of fire" will find that their lustful passions continue. We have reason to believe that these desires will be increased but without the possibility of satisfaction. We are reminded of the rich man in hades, who cried for a drop of water to cool his parched tongue. The wicked will be tormented by feelings of despair and unfulfilled longings. They will suffer from never-ending aloneness, with no one to hear their cries.

But for those who are raised to the resurrection of life, sinful urges shall vanish forever. In heaven we will serve God fully because we *want* to. We will not be tempted to do otherwise. Urges for revenge, greed, and sexual expression will no longer interfere with our unrestricted fellowship with God. Now every holy desire will be fulfilled, and we shall live in bliss and satisfaction.

The reason that our bodies must be transformed is because "flesh and blood cannot inherit the kingdom of God, nor does the perishable inherit the imperishable" (1 Corinthians 15:50). A temporary and decaying body is out of place in an environment of eternal and undiminished glory. That which is perishable cannot coexist with the imperishable.

This new spiritual body will not be a spirit. When the disciples met the risen Christ and feared that they had seen only a ghost, Jesus challenged them, "Look at my hands and my feet. It is I myself! Touch me and see; a ghost does not have flesh and bones, as you see I have" (Luke 24:39). Then He proceeded to show them His hands and His feet.

Let me say it plainly: The resurrection body is a *body*. It will be reconstituted with a different molecular structure, but a body it shall be. In fact, although we will not have to eat to live, eating will be a part of our eternal fellowship. We've noted that Jesus ate fish with His disciples along the shores of Galilee—and we will all be invited to the marriage supper of the Lamb!

Do you find all this difficult to grasp? That's not surprising, because, as Paul wrote, "No eye has seen, no ear has heard, no mind has conceived what God has prepared for those who love him" (1 Corinthians 2:9). An old story tells of a little girl who saw a picture book of Jesus and that night dreamed of heaven. The next morning she exclaimed, "Oh, Mother, He is so much more beautiful than the pictures!"

BURIAL OR CREMATION?

In this passage, Paul uses the analogy of a seed: "When you sow," he writes, "you do not plant the body that will be, but just a seed, perhaps of wheat or of something else. But God gives it a body as he has determined, and to each kind of seed he gives its own body" (1Corinthians 15:37–38). The fact that seeds are planted in the ground and then are resurrected to give life was one reason the early church buried their dead. They rejected the custom of cremation that was practiced in their culture, believing that Jesus' followers should adopt the model of His death, burial, and resurrection for themselves.

I approach this issue with caution, for I know many Christians who have chosen to be cremated rather than buried. Indeed, there are good arguments for cremation: We are running out of burial space; eventually, the buried body disintegrates anyway; cremation is cheaper, thus saving funds that could be used for better purposes. Certainly cremation seems to be wise in some instances where there is danger of the spread of disease and where burial options are impossible because of the location of the body, or the manner in which death occurred. On the fateful terrorist attacks on September 11, 2001, many hundreds of bodies were cremated without the consent of the victims or relatives.

That said, I believe that burial for the Christian is preferable to cremation. I do not believe that cremation is a sin, since the Scriptures do not forbid the practice, but there were reasons that both the Hebrews of the Old Testament and the Christians of the New Testament buried their dead.

First, the early Christians followed the example of Jesus and the saints in Jerusalem, such as Stephen, Ananias, and Sapphira, who were buried, not cremated. The Christians in Rome took the bodies of St. Justin and his companions and "buried them in a fitting place." This did not mean that the early Christians assumed that the resurrection was dependent on the preservation of the body, but burial was symbolic of the resurrection.

Second, the Christians believed that burial

better expressed the sanctity of the body. Since our bodies are created by God and through faith become the temple of the Holy Spirit (1 Corinthians 6:19–20), it was thought inappropriate to have the body destroyed by fire. The body was created from the dust, and the best way for it to return to dust was through the decomposition that sets in through burial. Fire in Scripture is often associated with God's judgment, not His blessing.

Third, we've already spoken of Paul's imagery that the body is like a seed sown in the ground. Like an acorn that will eventually be an oak tree, so the body is sown in the ground to arise in a new form. This metaphor, along with the New Testament's reference to the dead as "sleeping," is best depicted by burial, not cremation.

Interestingly, many non-Christian countries practice cremation, not merely for lack of burial space but because burning the body symbolizes the pagan notion that the body is to return to the unity of nature, or the great "One." In contrast, the practice of burial handles the body with tenderness in hope of its coming resurrection. During times of plague, the early church, where feasible, washed the bodies of unbelievers and buried them, arguing that even the wicked should have a proper burial in light of their own future resurrection.

As a pastor, I have had to deal with the matter of cremation. Whenever appropriate, I counsel

burial, but I have never made this a point of con-
tention if cremation is preferred. There are several
current burial practices I would like to see changed
to reduce the cost of burial and make it more con-
ducive to a Christian understanding of the body.
Those matters are best discussed in a different con-
text. Cremation is not inherently evil, but burial
follows the pattern of Jesus and the early church.

"I'M READY TO GO."

An eighty-something woman who had had her
share of cancer was rushed to the hospital for what
she thought would be her final ride. Her children
insisted that she be put on the most sophisticated
life supports, given the latest treatments to eke out
a few more days of miserable existence. When she
was able to speak she rebuked them, "Don't interfere with my glorification. . . . My bags are packed;
I'm ready to go."

For those who have received the gift of eternal
life, the redemption of the body motivates them to
accept death as the inevitable consequence of living in a fallen world. Whenever I'm asked to perform a graveside service for a believer, I always end
with these words, "And now we commit _____'s
body to its final resting place until the resurrection
of the Last Day." As Jesus was buried and rose

again, so His followers know that their bodies will rise to future glory.

> *When the perishable has been clothed with the imperishable, and the mortal with immortality, then the saying that is written will come true: "Death has been swallowed up in victory."*
>
> *"Where, O death, is your victory?*
> *Where O death, is your sting?"*
>
> *The sting of death is sin, and the power of sin is the law. But thanks be to God! He gives us the victory through our Lord Jesus Christ. Therefore, my dear brothers, stand firm. Let nothing move you. Always give yourselves fully to the work of the Lord, because you know that your labor in the Lord is not in vain.*
> (1 Corinthians 15:54–58)

The seed has been planted, but new life will spring forth when the trumpet sounds; and we who have died in Christ are raised to be reunited with our Savior—clad forever in our new bodies!

CHAPTER EIGHT

A MESSAGE TO THIS WORLD FROM MARS

I'm into spirituality but not organized religion."

I'd heard that many times before, but this time the declaration came from a woman who was reared in a strong evangelical church. She was disillusioned with the rigid teachings she had received since childhood and felt the need to explore other "religious options." She was "spiritual," she said, but not into any kind of theology. She wanted to keep her relationship with God private, undemanding, and according to her own schedule and tastes.

So do many other Americans and others in the "civilized" world. They dismiss ideas of doctrine and spiritual authority, wanting instead to be left

alone with their own god and enjoy the relationship on their own terms. Best-selling books explore
the relationship between spirituality and sex, spirituality and wealth, spirituality and health. Anthro-
pologists have found that a desire to connect with
the divine is hardwired into mankind, and in our
day this search is rampant—and often misguided.

Many spiritual seekers believe that everything
in the material world can be reduced to "spirit." To
discover the true meaning of life, we must, through
meditation, go deep within ourselves. There are
dozens of ways to access the spirit world from
which we can draw strength and wisdom, such
seekers believe. "You don't have to believe in anything except your own innate goodness and your
personal god's infinite capacity to accept you as
you are," they say.

This preoccupation with spirituality emerged
about three decades ago. Before that, the philosophy of materialism dominated the West—the notion that there are no gods, angels, or spirits of any
kind. The totality of all that existed was believed to
be matter; and everything, including the human
mind, could be reduced to physics and chemistry.
All religions were viewed as superstitions that
needed to be discarded in favor of the proven
results of scientific research. Perhaps Carl Sagan,
the late astronomer, best summed up this world-

view: "The cosmos," he stated, "is all there ever was and all there ever will be."

Faced with these competing philosophies, how can the follower of Jesus communicate the truth of Christ to our culture?

Standing on ancient Athens' Mars Hill, Paul confronted worldviews that approximate our contemporary ideas of spirituality and materialism. He has a word for those who believe that they are "spiritual but not into religion" and for those who reject the spiritual in every dimension of existence.

A JOURNEY TO THE TOP OF MARS HILL

Let's put history on rewind and meet the ancient philosophers who stood on Mars Hill; and let's hear Paul's word to them—and to us. We will discover that not much has changed throughout the centuries.

Meet the Philosophers

"A group of Epicurean and Stoic philosophers began to dispute with him. Some of them asked, 'What is this babbler trying to say?' Others remarked, 'He seems to be advocating foreign gods'" (Acts 17:18). The Epicurean philosophers were the materialists who denied the existence of the soul or spirit; they denied that there could be an invisible god who was not subject to natural law. They bore many similarities to the atheistic humanists of today.

Morally, the Epicureans were hedonists, believing that the ultimate purpose of life was pleasure. Given their view of the world, they did not believe in immortality or a final judgment. What we call the "soul" disintegrates into dust, and so death ends all conscious existence.

Though there may be variations in this philosophy, many people today are Epicureans, at least in a practical sense. Enjoy *this* world, they assert, because there is no world to come.

The Stoics, on the other hand, were pantheists who believed that "God is all and all is God." They believed in the immortality of the soul and the final absorption of the human soul into the divine. They believed that the ultimate reality of the universe was spiritual; thus, they were obsessed with astrology and spiritual experiences. For them, there was a coming future existence, though its form was unknown.

The Stoics believed in virtue for its own sake. For them, the highest good was the state of existence that was undisturbed by good and evil. Like the Hindus of today, they sought to be unmoved by either pleasure or pain. Even today we use the term "stoic" to denote someone who can endure the ups and downs of life without flinching.

In our day, we stand with Paul on Mars Hill. The materialists, who deny the existence of any spiritual reality, need to hear what we have to say. So do the "spiritual" seekers among us who believe in dozens of entry points into the spirit world, be they through angels or witches or other psychic phenomena.

Let's re-create the scene. Athens enjoyed freedom of religion and tolerated just about every spiritual opinion. You could believe in whatever god you liked; in fact, there were as many different kinds of gods as there were preferences among the people. And the people enjoyed discussing religion; for some it was a pastime, for others it was a matter of conviction and ego.

With the controversy stirring, Paul was brought to the Areopagus, the place we know as Mars Hill. This was the forum for discussion, dialogue, and argument. Here was the place where the educated Athenians would gather to debate the latest ideas. In this setting Paul would interpret the religious fervor of the city and speak of the Resurrection, arguing that God had personally broken into history with a revelation of Himself.

Revealing the Unknown God

Paul began by commending the Athenians. "Men of Athens! I see that in every way you are very religious" (Acts 17:22). I've always believed that we ought to commend people for seeking truth, even if they are looking in the wrong place and coming to wrong conclusions. This age, with its religious superstitions, its fascination with the occult, and its insistence on pluralism, gives us a bridge by which we can introduce the good news about Jesus. It is easier to witness to people who are searching for spiritual reality than it is to create an interest in those who are indifferent to any sort of spiritual concern.

Here's Paul's introduction: "For as I walked around and looked carefully at your objects of worship, I even found an altar with this inscription: TO AN UNKNOWN GOD. Now what you worship as something unknown I am going to proclaim to you" (v. 23). What a brilliant introduction! The Athenians believed in many gods, and because they feared they might have overlooked one or more of them, they built an altar to a god they might have excluded from the religious roster. Paul picked up on this and said he would reveal the God who was unknown to them—the God they were looking for.

Art Linkletter told the story of a boy who was drawing a sketch on a piece of paper. Linkletter asked the boy what he was drawing. "God," he replied. "But nobody knows what God is like," Linkletter replied. To which the boy responded, "They will when I get through!"

Needless to say, Paul was not going to draw a picture of God, but he was going to explain to the Athenians some of His characteristics and, even better, give them some evidence that He revealed Himself in Jesus Christ. If they listened carefully, they might come to know this unknown God.

His speech continued:

"The God who made the world and everything in it is the Lord of heaven and earth and does not live in temples built by hands. And he is not served by human hands, as if he needed anything, because he himself gives all men life and breath and everything else. From one man he made every nation of men, that they should inhabit the whole earth; and he determined the times set for them and the exact places where they should live." (vv. 24–26)

Paul introduced God as Creator to them. He wanted the philosophers in Athens to understand that "nature" could not account for what they saw around them. It is simply not true that "the cosmos is all there ever was, and all there ever will be," for the cosmos cannot have produced itself. God is independent of the world; we exist for Him; He does not exist for us. His glory and pleasure is all that matters.

Paul explained that the God who created the heavens is the same God who is personally available for the human race. If creation is evidence

of the transcendence of God—His otherness—
then His accessibility is proof of His immanence
—His nearness. "God did this so that men would
seek him and perhaps reach out for him and find
him, though he is not far from each one of us.
'For in him we live and move and have our being'"
(vv. 27–28).

The true God is not unapproachable, nor is He
only distantly related to His creation. One of the
most famous of the Athenians, Aristotle, had
taught that God was the prime mover of the universe, totally unaffected by what was happening
within the world. Though presenting a very different approach to philosophy, his pupil Plato also
taught that God could not have any direct contact
with the world. God, the Athenians believed, was
beyond all of our senses and experiences.

In contrast, Paul preached the accessibility of
God. To ask the question, "Where is God?" is like a
fish in the ocean asking where he can find water.
God is near to us, for we live and move in Him. The
New Agers are right when they assert that God is
open to contact and communication; they err in
thinking that we can connect with Him apart from
His personal revelation in Jesus Christ.

Of course, we must ask, "If God is so near, why
does He appear to be so far away?" Although there
is no *physical* distance between God and us, the
Bible is clear that there is *moral* distance between

us. This explains why God appears to be far away, even though He may be near at hand. With Job, we have all cried out, "If only I knew where to find him; if only I could go to his dwelling!" (23:3).

Paul tells the Athenians—and us—where they can find Him. He also gives them a warning.

PERSONAL GODS
VERSUS THE ONE TRUE GOD

A God After One's Own Image

Paul warned the Athenians about the notion of idolatry, the idea that we can fashion a god after our own image. We should not think that God is like an image of our own making, however skilled its creation. "In the past," Paul said, "God overlooked such ignorance, but now he commands all people everywhere to repent. For he has set a day when he will judge the world with justice by the man he has appointed. He has given proof of this to all men by raising him from the dead" (Acts 19:30–31).

The Athenians had a date with destiny. Whether they knew it or not, they would individually be brought into the presence of this "Unknown God" for judgment. The reason they should seek this God was not just for personal fulfillment but also because He would someday call them to account.

Responsibility in that Day of Judgment will be based on what people did with what they knew.

This judgment will be personal, detailed, and compulsory. No one will escape; no one will be able to get by with putting the best spin on his or her performance. When I was in Bible college I sang in a choir, and I got through the difficult parts by singing softly and letting the voices of those around me carry the words and tune. Just so, many people think that they will be able to hide behind others on the Day of Judgment or perhaps look better in comparison to those around them. But when God judges us, there will be no one to cover for us, no one to make us look better than we really are. In effect, we will be asked to sing a solo; our true motives and lifestyle will be open for inspection.

This thought of God's judgment is balanced by His mercy. Paul says God now "commands all people everywhere to repent." Something can be done about our predicament. We can make a decision today that will determine our eternal destiny. If we turn to God through Jesus Christ, we will discover Him to be just as near as the Bible says He is.

Though God might appear to be too high to get over, too deep to get under, and too complex to understand, He can be found if we seek Him through the one Man whom He has appointed— Jesus Christ. And there is proof that this is so.

The One and Only

Just yesterday, I discussed the Resurrection with a workman who did some repairs in our home. He said he believed in God—it was Jesus he could not accept. He respected Jesus, he told me, but he could not believe that He was the Son of God or the final religious authority in the world. After all, there are other religions that seem to be equally valid.

So what qualifies Jesus as Judge and Savior? Paul continued, "He has given proof of this to all men by raising him from the dead" (v. 31). The Resurrection is proof that God has entered our world; it validates Jesus' other claims to deity, His ability to forgive sins and receive worship. We have many people making religious claims, but only one Man was resurrected from the dead, proof that He conquered death and has given us assurance that we can be prepared to enter the life beyond. If getting crucified and raised from the dead were a requirement to begin a new religion, we would have fewer religions in the world—more accurately, we would have only *one* religion in the world.

The idols of the Athenians could not tell the people how to be reconciled to God, but Jesus, the God-man, can. Jesus stands alone in the pantheon of deities. None other has made such compelling claims to deity; none other predicted His death and resurrection. The better we understand Him, the more impossible it is to believe that He is just one among many others.

Yet humans are born with a seemingly irresolvable conflict: On the one hand, we are created for God and seek Him; on the other hand, we want to find Him in our own way and through our own intuitions.

God created the nations so that men and women would "reach out for him" (Acts 17:27). And so they do, but often they do not find Him. They seek Him in the wrong way and for the wrong reasons.

- They seek for God when they join a self-help seminar that teaches that they must go deep within themselves to find wholeness and meaning.
- They seek for God when they enter into an intimate relationship with a friend, hoping to find meaning and fulfillment.
- They seek for God when they pursue sex, drugs, and power to deaden the emptiness within.
- They seek for God when they enter into occult practices, hoping to connect with something greater than they are.
- They seek for God when they fill their lives with every kind of pleasure, so that they can ignore the deadening reality of a troubled conscience.

Paul's message: "Draw near to God through Christ." The One who will judge the world is now the One who is saving the world.

THE AUDIENCE RESPONSE

An interviewer would have soon discovered that opinions were divided in response to Paul's speech. Just as today, people had different reactions to the resurrection of Jesus.

The Mockers

First, there were those who mocked. "When they heard about the resurrection of the dead, some of them sneered" (v. 32). They said, in effect, "We can't believe this nonsense." The Epicureans did not believe in life after death; the Stoics believed that their souls would survive after death, but they did not believe in the resurrection of the body, so they joined in mocking the idea of Jesus' resurrection and the promise that He would judge the world.

Today Jesus is, for the most part, well thought of. He is admired as a Teacher, a prophet, and a guru who opens up divine reality for us. But He is not believed to be the only Savior and Judge of the world. If you were on a contemporary talk show and said, "Jesus has changed my life," the crowd would cheer. But if you were to say, "We can't be forgiven or come to know God except through Jesus," you would be booed.

But Jesus—the Jesus Paul preached—cannot be either ignored or put on the same shelf as Buddha, Krishna, and Muhammad. The witnesses to the Resurrection are plentiful and compelling. Five hundred people saw Christ alive, and many of them were still living when Paul wrote this letter to the congregation in Corinth.

Jesus was mocked at His first coming. Instead of a regal crown, they decked His brow with a twisted circle of thorns. Instead of a robe, they gave Him a shawl; and instead of a scepter, they gave Him a stick. "Hail, king of the Jews!" the soldiers shouted as they spat on Him (Mark 15:18).

No wonder some also mocked His resurrection. Peter predicted that many would scoff at the second coming of Christ to judge the world. "First of all, you must understand that in the last days scoffers will come, scoffing and following their own evil desires. They will say, 'Where is this "coming" he promised? Ever since our fathers died, everything goes on as it has since the beginning of creation'" (2 Peter 3:3–4).

Although some mock, we read that "God cannot be mocked" (Galatians 6:7). God is not in a hurry to settle His accounts—but in the end, the resurrected Christ will not be ignored. God says *today*, not tomorrow, is the day of salvation.

The Procrastinators

Second, others on Mars Hill delayed and said, "We want to hear you again on this subject" (Acts 17:32). They were not ready to make a decision, but they were open to investigation. Then, as now, people use the notion of "tolerance" to hold all religious opinions at arm's length. They tell themselves that they will revisit the issues, but they are not ready. The problem is that they are never ready!

Tomorrow looks innocent and appears quite certain. Yet we read, "Do not boast about tomorrow, for you do not know what a day may bring forth" (Proverbs 27:1). For those who delay, their eternal destiny is as uncertain as tomorrow. Actually, it is *more* uncertain; for it can be shown a thousand times that those who delay today also will delay tomorrow. Indecision about Christ is a clear decision to turn away from Him to our own understanding and desires.

George Sweeting, former Moody Bible Institute president, has said, "The road marked *tomorrow* leads to the town called *never.*" Tomorrow is not God's time; it is Satan's time. No one ever drifts to God; no one ever drifts to heaven. For the person who chooses to delay, there will never be enough evidence to believe. Sometimes those who intend to repent at 12:00 midnight die at 11:00 P.M.

Jesus told a parable about wise and foolish virgins. They were not anti-God or anti-bridegroom; they just neglected to get oil. "And while they were going away to make the purchase, the bridegroom came, and those who were ready went in with him to the wedding feast; and the door was shut" (Matthew 25:10 NASB). The five who did not have oil were good people, but they procrastinated. "Later the others also came. 'Sir! Sir!' they said, 'Open the door for us!' " (v. 11). But they were told that they were not on the reservation list. Neglect can damn you.

There's a legend of three demons who were overheard plotting how to win followers for their master. The first said, "Tell the people there is no God."

"No, that won't do," the others replied. "There are too many evidences of His goodness about."

The second proposed, "Say there is no hell."

"That won't convince people either, because some of their friends are already there."

The third suggested the most effective way: "Tell them there is no hurry."

The Believers

Thankfully, there was a third response that day on Mars Hill. We read, "A few men became followers of Paul and believed. Among them was Dionysius, a member of the Areopagus, also a woman named Damaris, and a number of others"

(Acts 17:34). They "believed" that is, they admitted that they were sinners in need of a Savior; they affirmed that Jesus was all He claimed to be.

CHRIST DEFEATED . . .

In 1815, the duke of Wellington commanded the victorious forces at the great Battle of Waterloo that ended the Napoleonic Wars. Apparently, when the battle was over, Wellington sent news of his victory to England. A series of stations, one within sight of the next, had been established to relay the message between the European continent and England. Fog set in, and only two words were seen, "Wellington Defeated." Discouragement spread throughout Britain as the news of the defeat arrived on the shore.

But when the fog lifted, the third word of the transmission appeared. The complete message read, "Wellington Defeated Napoleon."

We look at what happened on Good Friday and we see only two words, "Christ defeated . . ." But on the third day, we read the complete message, "Christ defeated death. . . ."

The message given on Mars Hill reminds us that amid the idols of our culture, God comes to us through Jesus, who was raised from the dead. Today He is our Savior, tomorrow our Judge, and eternally our Lord.

DYING IN HIS HANDS

The question is not whether we will die, but *how* we will die.

We can look to Jesus and His last moments on the cross as our example. He taught us how to live, but He also taught us how to die. He who went before us and showed us the way invites us to join Him in the world beyond. The darkness was forever over; the suffering was finished, and now He was finally able to commit His spirit into the hands of His Father, whose sweet presence had returned.

He left us the legacy of a "good death."

His last words in the flesh were, "Father, into your hands I commit my spirit" (Luke 23:46). He commended His spirit to the Father, placing Himself with assurance into the Father's care. And the good news is that you and I can die with the same confidence.

Interestingly, none of the New Testament writers is content to simply say that Jesus died; they all say that His spirit went into the hands of God. They want us to understand that His death was not the end but the beginning of a new relationship. If we learn from our Master, we will be ready when our final hour comes. He died in faith and was rewarded with the Resurrection, and so shall we.

In ancient times a "forerunner" would help a vessel enter the harbor safely. He would jump from the ship, wade to the harbor, and fasten the strong rope of the ship to a rock along a shore. Then by means of a winch, the vessel was brought in. This is the imagery used by the author of Hebrews, who views Jesus as the One who has gone to heaven to prepare the way for us. "We have this hope as an anchor for the soul, firm and secure. It enters the inner sanctuary behind the curtain, where Jesus, who went before us, has entered on our behalf." (Hebrews 6:19–20). Let storms tear our sails to shreds; let the floors creak; let the gusts of wind attempt to blow us off course; the redeemed shall arrive safely at port. Each day we are pulled a notch closer to the harbor by the One who has proved that He is stronger than death.

Jesus died according to the purposes of divine providence, not the whims of the envious religious leaders or cowardly Romans. Just so, you and I will die; not according to the will of cancer; not according to the will of an erratic drunk cruising along the highway; not according to the will of a painful disease. Any one of these might be the chariot God will use to take us to Himself, but be assured we will die under the good hand of God's providential care. We will pass through the curtain according to God's clock, not the timetable of random fate.

He Died in the Father's Hands

"Father, into your hands . . ."

What a world of meaning is locked in that expression!

There are two different kinds of hands mentioned in the Bible. Repeatedly, Jesus said He was being delivered up into the hands of men. To His weary disciples in Gethsemane, He said, "Look, the hour is near, and the Son of Man is betrayed into the hands of sinners. Rise, let us go! Here comes my betrayer!" (Matthew 26:45–46). Peter said that Jesus was crucified by "wicked men" (Acts 2:23). Wicked hands formed a crown of thorns and put it on His brow. Wicked hands lacerated His back; wicked hands slapped Him; and wicked hands shoved Him. Wicked hands put nails through His hands and feet.

But there came a time when the hands of men could do no more, and Jesus was left in the hands of His Father. Jesus voluntarily gave Himself into the hands of sinners—now He voluntarily gave Himself into the hands of God. Surrounded by those who hated Him, knowing that the injustices against Him were as yet unaddressed, knowing that His disciples had for the most part deserted Him— in these circumstances He could count on His Father to receive His spirit. In the Father's hands, He was elevated to a position of authority, and today is waiting for His enemies to become a footstool for His feet.

Note well: Jesus was just as committed to suffer in His Father's hands as He was to rejoice in His Father's hands. The hands that brought the suffering would now bring joy and relief. The first recorded words of Jesus were, "Do you not know that I must be about my Father's business?" (Luke 2:49). Now that His Father's business was finished, His last words would be, "Father, into your hands I commit my spirit." From beginning to end, this Son cared only about one thing: doing the Father's will and finishing it.

Jesus teaches us that death is the door by which we are admitted into the presence of the King. He also reminds us that it is possible to die young and yet to have fulfilled the will of God. The more closely we walk with God, the more easily we will believe that He can be trusted with our spirits— that part of us that is the seat of our thinking, willing, caring, and feeling. Yes, of course, we want to be buried, as proof of our belief in the resurrection. Regardless of what becomes of our body, our spirit can return safely home. Come what may, we too shall be welcomed into the inner sanctum of the Father's presence.

> *Plagues and deaths around me fly,*
> *Till He please I cannot die*
> *Not a single shaft can hit*
> *Till the God of love sees fit.*[1]

If we are in the hands of the Father, we are also in the hands of the Son. Earlier in His ministry Jesus said to His disciples, "My sheep listen to my voice; I know them, and they follow me. I give them eternal life, and they shall never perish; no one can snatch them out of my hand. My Father, who has given them to me, is greater than all; no one can snatch them out of my Father's hand. I and the Father are one" (John 10:27–30). The hands of the Father and the Son are in harmony. How comforting to know that we are held by both, for the hands of the Father and the Son are locked together.

How to Be Sure

If your spirit does not go into the hands of God for safekeeping, it will go into the hands of God for judgment. The same hands that speak of hope and comfort also speak of terror and punishment. We are warned, "It is a dreadful thing to fall into the hands of the living God" (Hebrews 10:31). The hands that are today outstretched, inviting us to receive mercy, are the hands that will throw the unrepentant into the pit of loneliness, despair, and the boredom of eternal suffering.

Before Timothy McVeigh was executed, he said he would have plenty of company in hell. One woman who was interviewed agreed that he would have company there with the likes of Hitler and Stalin. She was quite correct, but it would be a mistake to think that only such criminals will be in eternal punishment. Hell will be filled with many who paid their taxes, refused to commit immorality, and were never charged with a crime. In short, all those who do not come under the protection of Christ's righteousness will eventually be separated from Him in conscious torment. That explains why Jesus said that the way to life was narrow and "only a few find it" (Matthew 7:14).

Don't be wrong about whether or not you are in God's protective hands. When the early Reformer John Hus was condemned by the Council of Constance in 1415, the bishop ended the ceremony with the ominous words, "Now we commit your soul to the devil." But he replied, "I commit my spirit into thy hands, Lord Jesus Christ; unto thee I commend my spirit, which thou hast redeemed." Hus, who was a follower of Christ and understood the good news of the gospel, knew that no man can commit us into the hands of the devil if we have committed ourselves into the hands of God.[2] He was burned at the stake, triumphant in the knowledge that He belonged to Christ and Christ belonged to Him.

Perhaps you are thinking, *I will live as I please and then at the last minute I will say, "Father, into Your hands I commit my spirit."* No, with few exceptions, you will die as you have lived. If God is not your Father now, it might well be impossible to accept Him as your Father as death draws near. We are prepared for heaven when we embrace Christ as our sin bearer, accepting what He did on the cross for ourselves. Only those who so believe in Jesus can entrust their spirits to the Father with integrity.

SAFELY HOME

God does not promise a calm passage though the pathway of death, but He does promise a safe landing. Review once more the circumstances in which Jesus spoke these words. Those around Him jeered, denying Him the serene contemplation we would all want in our final moments. His body was bloody and crumpled; He was marred beyond recognition with ghastly scars and the contortions of dehydration. The pain numbed His body, and for a time, the Father's presence had left Him.

Yet His spirit was and is preserved. I've seen strong men dwindle down to a hundred pounds when cancer ravages their body. I've seen people so disfigured in auto accidents that the family was not allowed to view their body. I've read a story about a farmer caught in machinery and hacked to bits. Yes, some do die peacefully in a hospital room, or even at home surrounded by friends. But multitudes die violent deaths; others are lost in the ocean or die unheralded in remote jungles.

The promise is that no matter how turbulent the death, we will arrive safely at our destination. We have the sure knowledge that the spirit survives the body, and thanks to the Resurrection, our decaying bodies shall be raised to newness of life. We will be the same people in heaven as we are on earth. Yes, of course, sin will be removed, but we will carry our memories into the next life; we will also be aware of the attachments, friends, and relatives we had here.

Never shall the Cross and Resurrection be so precious to us as when death is near. For if we have embraced the Christ who died for us, we shall never really die. For He died, not merely that our sins would be taken away, but to prove that death does not have the last word for those whose faith is in the One who conquered it. "Since the children have flesh and blood, he too shared in their humanity so that by his death he might destroy him who holds the power of death—that is, the devil—and free those who all their lives were held in slavery by their fear of death" (Hebrews 2:14–15).

When the stones began to fly, Stephen, the first Christian martyr, prayed, "Lord Jesus, receive my spirit" (Acts 7:59). This is the only time in the New Testament that we read that Jesus was "standing at the right hand of God" ready to receive His servant. He is there waiting for us as well. When D. L. Moody was dying, he said, "Earth is receding, heaven is opening; if this be death, it is glorious."

The fact of Christ's resurrection gives us hope as we face death, not because we are blind to its horrors but because we look with confidence upon our trusted Savior. The Resurrection is the Great Reversal, the one reality that gives us the assurance that no other realities of our existence need ever permanently discourage us. "The Resurrection," said A. W. Tozer, "demonstrates once and for all who won and who lost."

Our faith is open to investigation. We do not give religious truth a privileged position, immune from rational evidence. There are good reasons to believe that God has entered our world.

We are invited to trust the One who conquered death.

If you have never trusted Christ as your Savior, I urge you to do so now. Tell Him that you are transferring all of your trust to Him as your personal sinbearer. His promise is that, for those who believe, eternal life awaits. Then you can die with His words on your lips:

"Father, into your hands I commit my spirit."

Prayer:

"O God, I know I am a sinner. But I thank You that Your Son Jesus died and was raised from the dead to save sinners. So I receive Him as my sin-bearer; I accept Him as having died for me.

"Thank You for the free gift of salvation that You have made available; it is a gift I now receive by faith."

"Yet to all who received him, to those who believed in his name, he gave the right to become children of God."
John 1:12

Portions of this chapter first appeared in Erwin W. Lutzer, Cries from the Cross *(Chicago: Moody, 2002), chapter 7.*

NOTES

Chapter 1: When Terror Fled

1. William McNeill, *Plagues and Peoples* (Garden City, N.Y.: Doubleday, 1976), 108.

2. Quoted in Rodney Stark, *The Rise of Christianity* (San Francisco: Harper San Francisco, 1997), 81.

3. Ibid.

4. James Montgomery Boice in Philip Ryken, "Moses in the Wilderness," audio recording, Tenth Presbyterian Church, Philadelphia, 7 May 2000. Available as tape C-000507T through the Alliance of Confessing Evangelicals, 215-546-3696.

5. Ibid.

6. Alice Meynell "Untitled," as cited in Leonard Sweet, *Homiletics* 2, no. 8 (April/June, 1996), 6.

7. As quoted in John Warwick Montgomery, *History and Christianity* (Downers Grove, Ill.: InterVarsity, 1971), 77–78.

8. "Because He Lives." Words by William J. Gaither and Gloria Gaither. Copyright © 1971 William J. Gaither, Inc. All rights controlled by Gaither Copyright Management. Used by permission.

9. W. Frank Harrington, "The One Who goes Ahead," *Preaching*, March/April 1999, 8.

10. Quoted in John Gladstone, *A Magnificent Faith* (Nova Scotia: Lancelot Press, 1983), 48.

Chapter 2: The Friend Who Calls Our Name

1. As quoted in James Montgomery Boice, *The Christ of the Empty Tomb* (Chicago: Moody, 1985), 60.

2. Quoted in Floyd Thatcher, ed., *The Miracle of Easter* (Waco, Tex.: Word, 1980), 31.

3. Jennie Evelyn Hussey, "Lead Me to Calvary." In public domain.

Chapter 3: How Jesus Resurrects Our Dreams

1. Quoted in *Preaching*, March/April 1999, 10, author unknown.

2. Alfred H. Ackley, "He Lives." © 1933 Word Music, LLC. All rights reserved. Used by permission.

Chapter 4: Can You Believe and Still Doubt?

1. George Matheson, *Portraits of Bible Men* (Grand Rapids: Kregel, 1987), 42–43.

2. George Matheson, "O Love That Wilt not Let Me Go." In public domain.

3. Charlotte Elliott, "Just As I Am." In public domain.

NOTES

†

Chapter 5: The Keeper of the Keys

1. William Shakespeare, *Hamlet,* act iii, scene 1, as quoted on the Internet at www.bartleby.com/100/138.32.html (excerpt 109). Accessed on 20 August 2003.

2. Erwin Lutzer, *One Minute After You Die* (Chicago, Moody, 1997), 78. The story was first recorded by Judson B. Palmer, who preceded Sandborn as pastor in a church in Iowa.

3. Ibid.

Chapter 6: Dying in the Care of Jesus

1. C. H. Spurgeon, *The Treasury of the Bible,* vol. 2 (Grand Rapids: Zondervan, 1962), 456.

2. Ibid., 457.

3. William Barclay, *The Daily Study Bible,* The Gospel of John, vol. 2 (Edinburgh: Saint Andrew Press, 1995 ed.), 110.

Chapter 7: Your Resurrection Body

1. Walter B. Knight, *Knight's Master Book of Ilustrations* (Grand Rapids: Eerdmans, 1956), 555.

Epilogue: Dying in His Hands

1. Quoted in C. H. Spurgeon, *The Treasury of the Bible,* vol. 2 (Grand Rapids: Zondervan, 1962), 119.

2. James Montgomery Boice, *The Christ of the Empty Tomb,* (Chicago: Moody, 1985), 65.

Since 1894, Moody Publishers has been dedicated to equip and motivate people to advance the cause of Christ by publishing evangelical Christian literature and other media for all ages around the world. Because we are a ministry of the Moody Bible Institute of Chicago, a portion of the proceeds from the sale of this book go to train the next generation of Christian leaders.

If we may serve you in any way in your spiritual journey toward understanding Christ and the Christian life, please contact us at www.moodypublishers.com.

"All Scripture is God-breathed and is useful for teaching, rebuking, correcting and training in righteousness, so that the man of God may be thoroughly equipped for every good work."
—2 Timothy 3:16, 17

MOODY
PUBLISHERS

THE NAME YOU CAN TRUST®

Cries from the Cross

The crucifixion of Jesus Christ brings us face to face with two seemingly contrary attributes of God—His love and His wrath, with two seemingly contradictory doctrines—the sovereignty of God and the free will of man. Once we understand Calvary, we can understand what it is to deny ourselves, take up our cross daily, and follow Him. This is a work we should all read.

Kay Arthur
Precept Ministries

ISBN: 0-8024-1111-8

Who Are You to Judge?

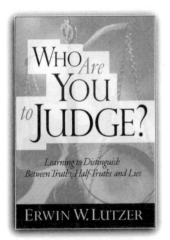

ISBN: 0-8024-0906-7

Who Are You to Judge? is a book about discernment; the ability to distinguish the false from the true, or better, the false from the half-true.

The crying need of the church today is for discernment—the ability to recognize truth and distinguish it from error. Who Are You to Judge? reminds us that truth is important, and (contrary to the spirit of our age) real truth is not merely a matter of subjective individual opinion.

John MacArthur

MOODY
PUBLISHERS

THE NAME YOU CAN TRUST.

1-800-678-6928 www.MoodyPublishers.org

THE VANISHING POWER OF DEATH TEAM

ACQUIRING EDITOR:
Greg Thornton

COPY EDITOR:
Jim Vincent

BACK COVER COPY:
Anne Perdicaris

COVER DESIGN:
Ragont Design

INTERIOR DESIGN:
Ragont Design

PRINTING AND BINDING:
Quebecor World Book Services

The typeface for the text of this book is
Giovanni